CONTEMPORARY PATCHWORK Quilts

"Solar Energy"

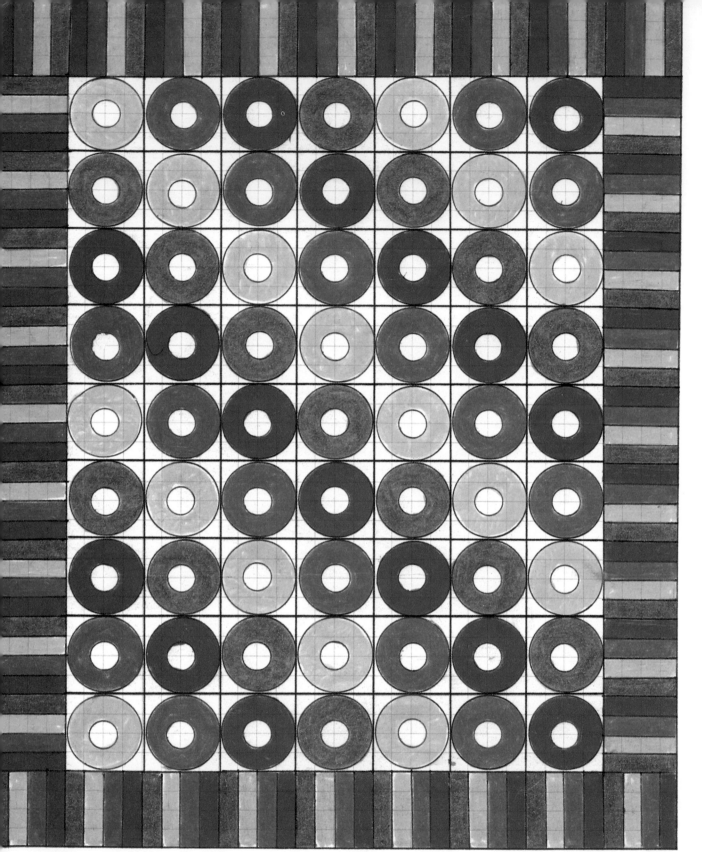

"Lifesavers"

CONTEMPORARY PATCHWORK
Quilts:
A STITCH IN OUR TIME

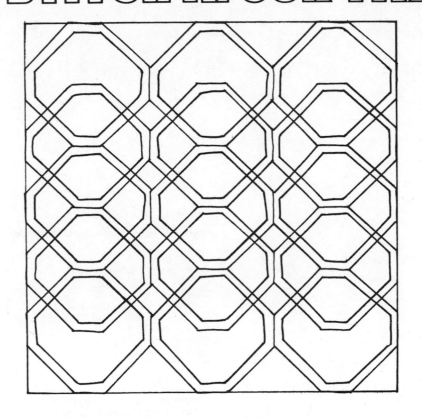

CONNIE MAJOR

 Sterling Publishing Co., Inc. New York

Dedicated with love to my family

Library of Congress Cataloging in Publication Data

Major, Connie.
  Contemporary patchwork quilts.

  Includes index.
  1. Quilting. 2. Patchwork. I. Title.
TT835.M343 1982   746.9'7   82-50545
ISBN 0-8069-5472-8
ISBN 0-8069-5473-6 (lib. bdg.)
ISBN 0-8069-7634-9 (pbk.)

Copyright © 1982 by Sterling Publishing Co., Inc.
Two Park Avenue, New York, N.Y. 10016
Distributed in Australia by Oak Tree Press Co., Ltd.
P.O. Box K514 Haymarket, Sydney 2000, N.S.W.
Distributed in the United Kingdom by Blandford Press
Link House, West Street. Poole, Dorset BH15 1LL, England
Distributed in Canada by Oak Tree Press Ltd.
% Canadian Manda Group, 215 Lakeshore Boulevard East
Toronto, Ontario M5A 3W9
Manufactured in the United States of America
All rights reserved

contents

"Log Cabin" is one of the most popular of traditional designs.

Early American Quilting

Traditional American patchwork quilts are like picture books of history. Economics, fashion, family, friends, superstitions, games, places, events, objects, politics, religion, social concerns, and nature have inspired the creation of hundreds of patchwork patterns throughout the past three centuries. Through the use of fabrics, colors, designs, and names given to them, women (and men) have described their everyday interests and surroundings, revealing aspects of our past that the history books sometimes overlook.

The first quilts made in America were for immediate protection against the harsh New England winters. Although the settlers brought quilts and quilting know-how from their European homelands, there was no time or material for creative sewing efforts. Survival took all their energy.

Since there was no ready supply of new fabric available to the early colonists, it's most likely that they utilized old clothing in the most economical way possible to obtain warm bedding. Although none of these earliest quilts have survived, they probably resembled crazy quilts with patches of any usable scraps of clothing sewn together to cover thinning spots in the bedding, with little concern for color or design. But with their sense of thrift and practicality, they laid the groundwork for the development of American patchwork design as we have come to know it today.

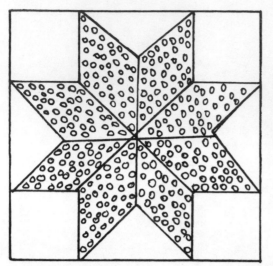

"LeMoyne Star" is one of the oldest of the named American patterns. It was named after the LeMoyne brothers who founded the city of New Orleans. The name was gradually Americanized to "Lemon Star." There are dozens of star, lily, and tulip patterns derived from this basic 8-point star.

The extreme hardships of the colonists were aggravated by the laws England clamped down on them regarding fabric. It was illegal for the colonists to manufacture their own fabric. They could buy textiles only from England. It was even illegal for anyone knowledgeable in textile skills to emigrate to America, under the threat of imprisonment when caught the first time and loss of hand (or head) the second.

These efforts by England to protect her textile trade monopolies motivated the colonists to pass their own laws to encourage America's cloth industry. Sheep were nurtured and protected by law. In some colonies, women and children were required to spin a certain amount of flax each day. Smugglers helped the cause by providing flax seed and sheep.

Through these actions, the colonists helped counteract the laws of England, though there still was not enough fabric to adequately clothe the entire colonial population, let alone make beautiful quilts. It took about a hundred years and the Industrial Revolution before steady supplies of fabric became available.

Even after fabric became more abundant, practicality still governed the actions of the colonists. Every salvageable bit of fabric from worn clothing or dressmaking continued to be collected in scrapbags kept in most households. Through these scrapbags the creative energies of women were channelled. Combining craftsmanship, artistic vision, and thrift, they began to develop a uniquely

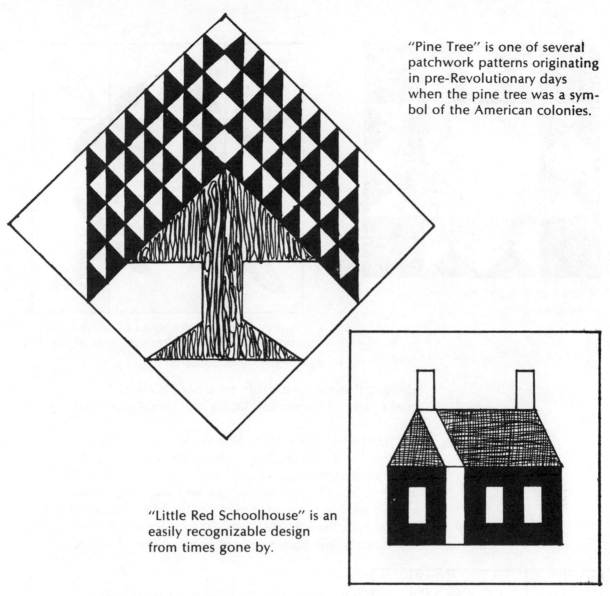

"Pine Tree" is one of several patchwork patterns originating in pre-Revolutionary days when the pine tree was a symbol of the American colonies.

"Little Red Schoolhouse" is an easily recognizable design from times gone by.

American way of viewing and expressing their world in patchwork quilts.

Most traditional American patchwork quilts are built up from pieces of fabric sewn together forming a basic geometric pattern or unit that is repeated block by block throughout the quilt resulting in the overall design. Although knowledge of quilting goes back to the ancient Egyptians and continues through history this patchwork design concept is uniquely American.

Some of these geometrically pieced patchwork patterns look very much like the source of the design. "Little Red Schoolhouse" and "Pine Tree" are but two of the many

"Crown of Thorns" has a religious theme.

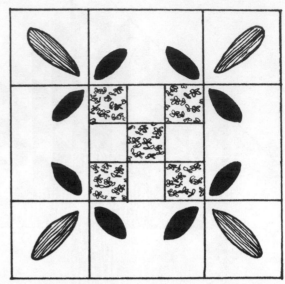

"Honey Bee" is also known as "Blue Blazes," a popular slang term from the end of the 19th century.

designs that were probably translated directly from the actual source of inspiration into a repeatable, geometric design.

Other designs are more abstract such as "Crown of Thorns" and "Honey Bee." They may have been consciously designed to express these aspects of the quiltmaker's life. Or, perhaps the pattern was created purely from a natural sense of design (or by what happened to be available in the scrapbag) with the design itself inspiring the name as the abstracted similarities were discovered.

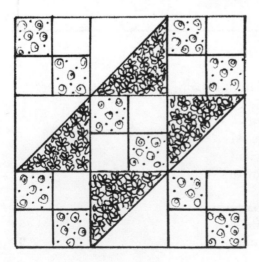

"Jacob's Ladder," a favorite prerevolutionary pattern of religious significance, was changed to "Road to Oklahoma" as the move West began. The name was changed again to "Road to California," obviously by women who were on the road to California. This same pattern came to be known during Civil War times in parts of the North as "The Underground Railroad." "Trail of the Covered Wagon," "Trail of Benjamin's Kite," "Stepping Stones," and "Wagon Tracks" are other names for the same basic design.

"54-40 or Fight" was a popular slogan in the 1830s and 1840s. It referred to a boundary dispute with Canada over the Pacific Northwest.

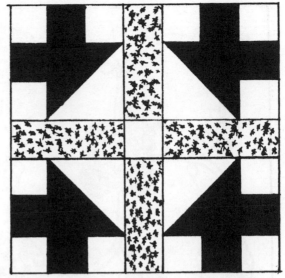

"Lincoln's Platform" commemorates the Lincoln-Douglas debates of 1854. There is also a patchwork design, referring to Douglas, called "The Little Giant."

Still other quilts were named to commemorate historical or political events, with the particular name giving direction to an interesting but objectively unrecognizable design. "Burgoyne Surrounded," "54-40 or Fight," and "Lincoln's Platform" are a few of these hundreds of designs that were given life because they were associated with meaningful aspects of their makers' lives.

As the surroundings and concerns of Americans changed, so did the names of their quilts.

Distinctive styles of patchwork developed in differing geographic locations as well. The strong, fundamental patchwork designs of the German settlers in Pennsylvania were reflections of their strong, fundamental religion. They often used several large pieces of fabric, as opposed to the thrifty New Englanders who used many small fabric scraps. Thus, New England patchwork patterns are apt to be more intricate than the broad Pennsylvanian ones.

Meanwhile the Southerners were making appliqué quilts. These were not a strong part of the origins of quilt design in this country because appliqué (sewing fabric cutouts on top of a background fabric) took extravagant use of fabric and time which was not available initially to the Northerners. However, the Southerners were wealthy

This is one of the many versions of "Whig Rose," also known by other names, depending on the maker's political persuasion.

and with spare time on their hands they could afford to put efforts into creating beautiful appliqué works.

As people began to push westward, their quilts were naturally more primitive than those made at the same time by New Englanders settled comfortably at home. The need for warm, durable bedcovers to be made as economically as possible was felt again.

Colors were as strong a vehicle for expression as the patchwork patterns they were made up into. The original quiltmakers used colors much as we do today—to reveal moods and feelings, celebrate fashions, and create something beautiful. In doing so, they inadvertently painted for us an additional picture of our past.

In any age, fashions come and go. Since quilts are made from the same stuff as clothing, it follows that fashions in quilts would come and go also. This has been true in the history of American quilts. Chintz, an imported cotton fabric, enjoyed tremendous popularity at one time. Scraps of it were cherished, with entire quilts designed around them. In the late eighteenth and early nineteenth centuries, scenes of historical events [such as the Louisiana Purchase] were printed on cottons, finding their way both into quilts and on the walls. Dark, flowered prints were widely used during the Civil War. Overdone, embroidered

"Sugar Loaf" originated in the days when sugar came wrapped in blue paper for shipment before it was granulated. The paper was often saved to use in dyeing fabric blue.

silk and velvet crazy quilts were a fad during the Victorian era—reflecting the excess and extravagance of the times.

It has long been known that colors correspond to feelings. Reds are stimulating; blues and greens, cool and relaxing; yellows and oranges, warm and cheerful; black, depressing; with hundreds of variations and subtleties in between. It is interesting to note that quilts made during the Depression and other hard times are noticeably more sombre and subdued than the brighter, gay quilts made during better times.

Quilts were colored by regional differences as well, reflecting the particular location, period, and beliefs of the people who lived there. German settlers in Pennsylvania developed a distinctive style of using colors. Their religion forbade them to use printed fabric, so creativity was brought to the forefront through color. Their rich, bold color combinations are striking, sometimes outrageous, but always beautiful. By contrast New England quilts are subdued. Colors were blended more conservatively. Southerners more often selected pastels for their pretty appliqué quilts.

Colors were also used to portray things both realistically (green for leaves, yellow for the sun) and symbolically. For example, "Rising Sun" was first done in the colors of the Continental Army's uniform. (It's easy to understand the symbolism in the name of this patchwork pattern for a struggling but hopeful new country.)

Quilts have always been adapted to satisfy the various and changing needs to their makers, wherever they were. Women made quilts to supply bedding not otherwise available. They created patchwork designs to provide the, sometimes, only bright spot of color and beauty to be found in a lonely, drab cabin. Quilts became a reason for which women could gather socially, via the quilting bee. For many, quilting bees were the only opportunity they had for getting together with friends and neighbors. Since quilting was one of the very few mediums available to women through which they could express themselves, they developed the art and craft beautifully, deeply, and sensitively.

It has been this ability of women to adapt patchwork quilting to the ever-changing times that has kept the art alive, dynamic, and meaningful throughout the history of this country. Of course, the urgent physical need for quilts, as in the lives of the colonists and pioneers, no longer exists. The need for self-expression however, has remained as an unbroken thread throughout the years. The patchwork quilt, as a vehicle for self-expression, is continually energized as it fulfills this need.

"Delectable Mountains" was inspired by a passage in the once popular *Pilgrim's Progress* by John Bunyan, "They went then, til they came to the Delectable Mountains, . . . to behold the gardens and orchards, the vineyards, and fountains of water. . . ."

14

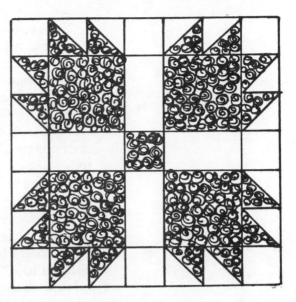

A very old pattern "Bear's Paw," as it was known in New England, meant more to women dealing with crows in their central Illinois cornfields as "Crow's Foot." The pattern was also known in Long Island as "Duck's Foot in the Mud," referring to the ducklings bred there since the days of the early Dutch settlers. This same design found meaning with the Philadelphia Quakers as "Hands of Friendship."

"Red Cross" was probably designed in honor of that association.

The same energy that was generated three centuries ago has exploded recently into a revival of interest in patchwork quilting. Quilting supplies with how-to books and magazines are readily available. Both men and women share in the development of contemporary quilting, whereas, in the past, quilting was predominantly a woman's art. Old-fashioned, time-consuming quilting methods have been revised to fit more realistically into today's fast-paced life-styles. Modern fabrics give new visual impact to old designs. And with the support of modern art authorities, traditional quilts can now stand on their own as valid, intense, and dynamic works of art.

However, in order to continue the spirit of patchwork, the sources of inspiration for our modern quilts must be updated too. "Goose Tracks," "Whig Rose," and "Lincoln's Platform" are traditional patterns, which may be interesting to us as designs, but the inspiration for them is far removed from our lives. We are much more apt to run into a "Cloverleaf Expressway" or a "Tract Homes" than a "Trail of the Covered Wagon" or a "Little Red Schoolhouse." It is difficult to relate personally to an "Indian Hatchet," but "Red Tape" or "No Deposit, No Return" are aspects of modern life that affect everyone. And who remembers the significance of "Churn Dash," "Sugar Loaf," and "Burgoyne Surrounded"? But then, who living 150 years ago could possibly understand today's "Product Code," "Nuclear Power Plants," or "McDonald's Arches"?

Modern patchwork designs continue to provide vehicles for self-expression. Some designs are celebrations of beauty and interests in our lives today. Others are expressions of present concerns and frustrations. They also reintroduce a way of seeing things that our ancestors discovered, which transforms some of the mundane, cold, or not-so-beautiful aspects of life into warm, human creations and, perhaps, makes them more bearable. Most importantly, these patterns can stimulate new, meaningful design ideas. Our world may seem very removed from that of our ancestors. However, with guidance from the past, we can discover interesting designs in our present world, create lasting heirlooms of beauty, and carry on the quilting tradition as well.

The Art of Design

Quilts are usually begun in one of two ways: Either you have a fabric scrapbag and a desire to make a quilt from it but no idea for a pattern, or else you have a design in mind but are at a loss for translating it into fabric. In either case, the following suggestions will help you to actualize your quilt.

If you have even the bare beginnings of a design idea, try drawing it on graph paper. I usually find that by working the idea into a repeatable, geometric form to somehow fit onto the graph-paper grid, the design will be more effective than trying to capture a lot of detail.

For example, "No Deposit, No Return" started out from the idea of pop bottles. The first drawing was of a bottle as I realistically saw it. I wasn't especially happy with the drawing, but it was a starting point for a good design I knew was there somewhere. I tried repeating the bottle which made things look worse. The space between the bottles was empty and meaningless. The bottles would be difficult to piece because there were no straight lines. I then repeated a few rows of bottles, but still the design had no particular movement or dynamics to it.

A few drawings later I realized that by changing the detailed curves of the bottles to a straight-line form, I would be closer to the visual effect I was after. It would also be easier to piece. I continued to experiment with a few different bottle sizes and arrangements until I was satisfied with the design. Seeing the bottles piled on top of each other suggested that the name be changed from "Bottles" to the more descriptive, meaningful, "No Deposit, No Return."

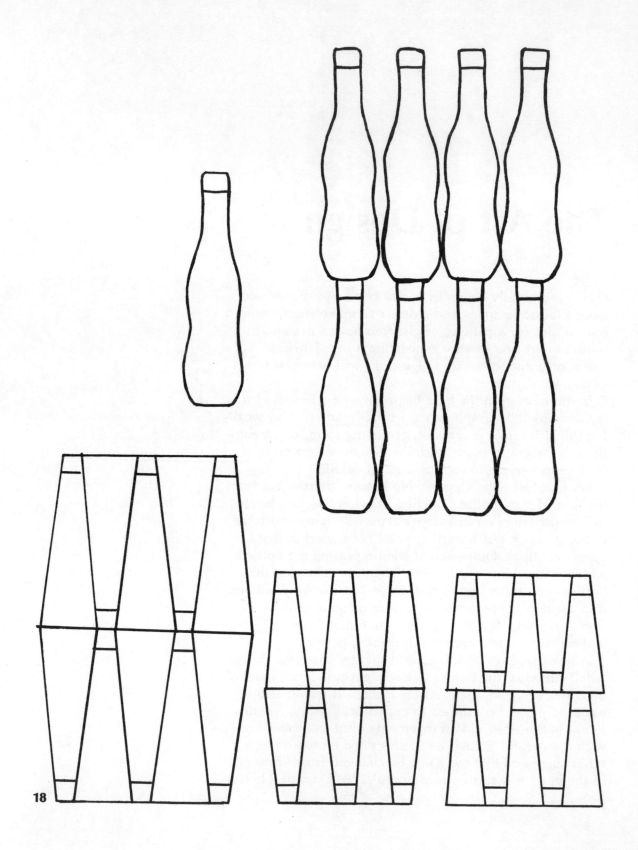

18

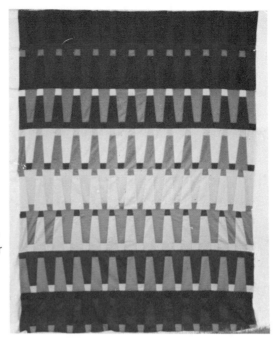

On the opposite page you can see how the shape of a soft-drink bottle was gradually changed and stylized until it provided the design for "No Deposit, No Return," on right.

"Product Code," the quilt shown bottom right, on the other hand, went through very little of an evolutionary process. The source of its inspiration is evident.

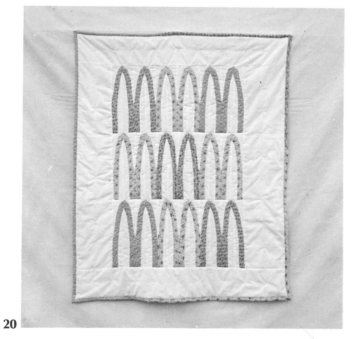

"Hamburger" (above) came before that other great American invention, "McDonald's Arches" (left), but the two were clearly made for each other.

"Dieter's Fruit Plate" (above) and
"Vegetarian" (right) offer contrast.

Three modern demons: "Morning Coffee" (top), "Sugar Blues" (left), and "Cigarettes" (above).

In addition to experimenting with graph paper, folding paper in various ways or arranging geometric cut-outs from construction paper can help formulate your design ideas, too. Doodling, coloring, and looking at colors and designs in fabrics can stimulate and organize your thoughts, whether you begin with an initial design idea or not.

In general, the simplest designs are the most effective. Intricate patchwork patterns are not necessarily the most beautiful. When designing your quilt, be aware that 90-degree angles and straight seams are the easiest to piece accurately. Hexagons, curved seams, and odd angles are difficult to maneuver and may be frustrating if undertaken as a first quilting endeavor. It is a better idea to have a simple but well thought out plan that you can complete successfully than an unfinished quilt—no matter how impressive the design on paper may be.

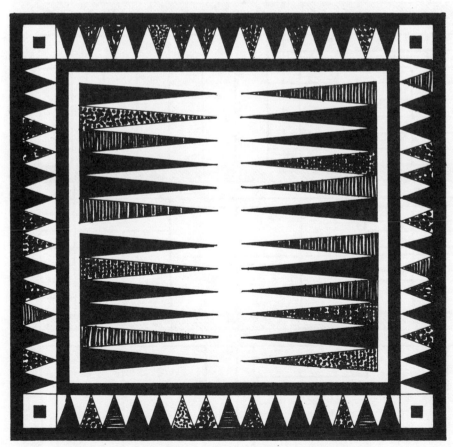

As you might guess, the title of this quilt is "Backgammon."

Although "No Deposit, No Return" began with the *concept* of bottles, sometimes it's the actual visual impact of repeated patterns that will trigger an idea. The numerous shelves of repeated geometric patterns to be found in a supermarket is one such example.

To begin the actual designing process, I drew the supermarket shelves as I remembered them, watching to see what sorts of patterns emerged. (See the full-page illustration on the facing page.) Choosing one section, which looked interesting to me, I enlarged it (see below), and then started experimenting with a variety of lights and darks. The result of this experimentation was a simple, but nice design. (See page 26.)

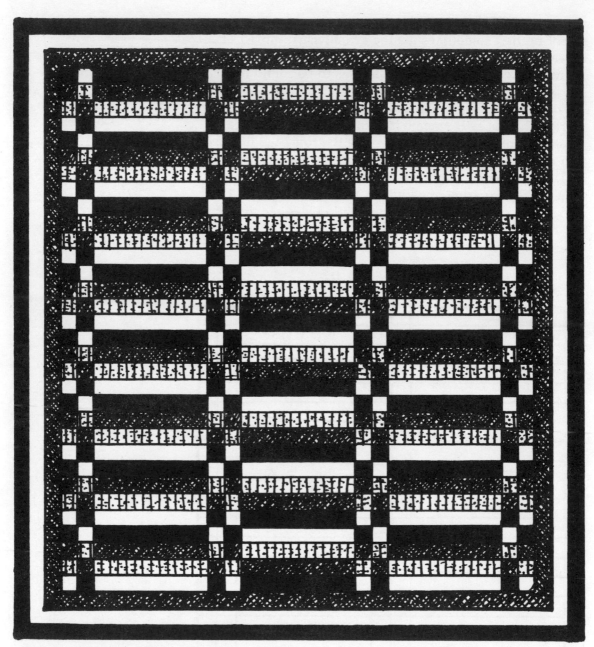

"Supermarket Shelves"

"Potted Plants"

Seek out as many quilts as possible. Study their construction. Note how the colors were used, and how you personally respond to them. Also, be aware of how the elements in each block work together—is there movement? Symmetry or asymmetry? Simplicity? Confusion? Contrast? See how the quilting complements—or conflicts—with the patchwork top.

Envision what you would like your finished quilt to look like before you actually cut any fabric out. It can be helpful to draw the entire quilt on graph paper, block-by-block. Sometimes, in the repetition of the blocks, a new pattern emerges that you will not have noticed before. One such example is "Back to Nature." The original drawing is shown on the opposite page. By joining the single blocks, a new tree design is formed, which you will see in color on page 39.

While designing your quilt, think about what size you want it translated into, depending on the size of your bed or wall space. To avoid working with fractions, I usually think in terms of each square on the graph paper as representing either one or two inches. Then I adjust the number of blocks in the quilt to fit approximately the desired dimensions, remembering to include any borders in the final measurement.

Always make at least one practice square before going ahead and cutting the pieces for your entire quilt. It would be a shame to have done all that work just to discover that your templates weren't accurately measured or cut out. A practice square will give you a chance to see how your color scheme is working, too. It will provide the opportunity to see if you enjoy piecing that particular pattern— and the best way to go about it.

Design your quilt with thought and care. With all the work that goes into it, you owe it to yourself to put a good deal of time into the planning stage as well. This way you will be less apt to change your mind midway through a project—possibly making more work for yourself by undoing your first idea to replace it with a better one. Sometimes though, despite the best of careful planning, a quilt takes on a life of its own, growing in ways impossible to predict. Spontaneity is part of quiltmaking too.

The technical aspects of designing a quilt are fairly easy to describe. But, as with most art forms, it is difficult to

"Back to Nature"

pin down exactly where the inspiration for specific designs came. The ideas for designs come from all directions, from many moods, for many reasons.

Sometimes I went out walking, consciously looking for repeated, geometric patterns in my neighborhood to redo into a quilt. It became an interesting challenge to try mentally to transform something as obnoxious as a crowded parking lot into a nice quilt.

Most of the quilts were not planned to look like a detailed photograph of the source of the design. Rather, the source served as a point of departure—a place to begin, but not necessarily end up at.

Some designs did in fact turn out looking like the original inspiration for·them, as for example, "Backgammon" and "Hamburgers." (See pages 23 and 20.) Others were more of a reaction against the source, as the translation of a hard-lined modern building into a soft construction of corduroy and velvet. ("Modern Architecture," page 60).

Actual experiences triggered the creation of a few quilts as well. The idea for "Sugar Blues" hit in the middle of a

Here the quilt "Sidewalk Bricks" has been photographed against a background of the sidewalk bricks that inspired it.

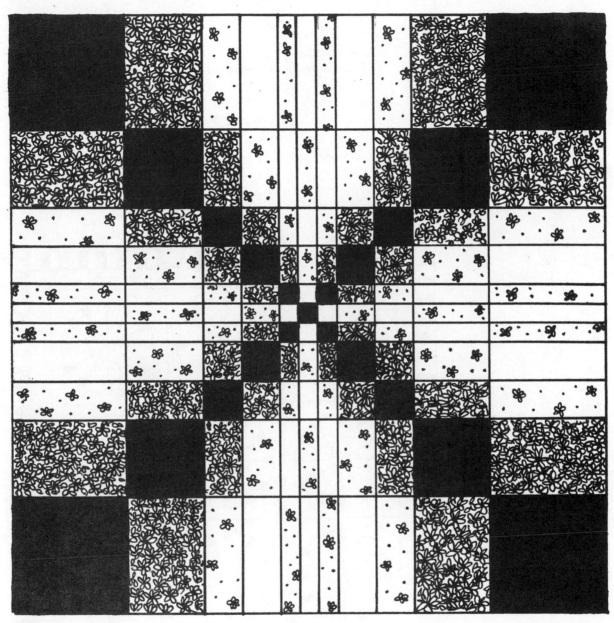

"Inflation"

candy bar binge. "Morning Coffee" developed during a
time I was in a routine of going out for coffee every morning. Thoughts for "Inflation" occurred when I was walking
home from the store with only half the groceries I had
planned on buying.

There are many available sources for design ideas that are easy to overlook because they are not particularly spectacular. They are just parts of our everyday lives, not old, not new, not controversial—mundane things, such as crossword puzzles or telephone wires. The original quilt-makers took some of their humdrum artifacts, such as spools and bow ties and used them as motifs for quilts. Now it's our turn.

The seasons, too, are part of our everyday lives—an all-important part. They were the inspiration for many quilts

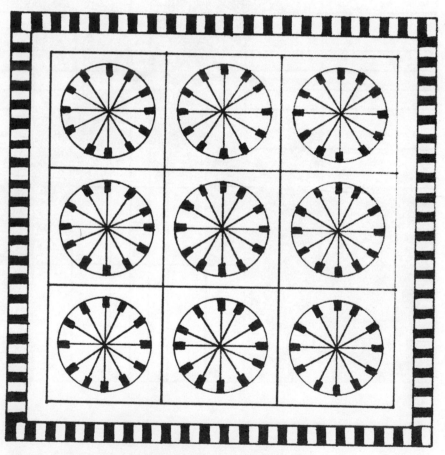

"Timepiece" is an appliqué quilt. Though stylized, the quilt could be described as representational rather than symbolic.

in the past and continue to be an inspiration today. "Spring Flowers" (page 35), "Sun Blossoms" (page 94, in color), "Vegetarian" (or "Autumn Harvest," in color on page 21), and "Winter Tree" on page 34 are a few examples.

A number of my designs have been inspired by the geometric patterns of modern architecture. There are, in

"Telephone Wires"

"Winter Tree"

"Spring Flowers"

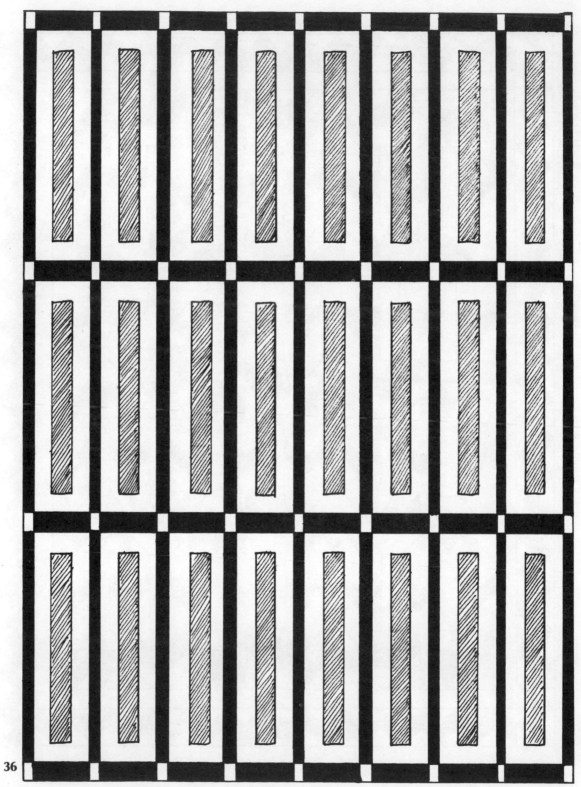

36

"Modern Architecture I"

fact, four designs by that name in this book: "Modern Architecture I" (on the opposite page), "Modern Architecture II," "Modern Architecture III," and "Modern Architecture IV." "Highrise Apartments," shown below is another one that owes its inspiration to that particular source.

"High-rise Apartments" is a simple, straight-seamed design, which uses "Sidewalk Bricks" as the border.

There are so many things in our lives today, which for better or worse, we cannot ignore. Nuclear power plants, red tape, or computer cards that we are not supposed to bend, fold, or mutilate—they are there—an all-pervasive part of our lives, therefore, affecting us somehow.

But the worst problems are caused by what we do to ourselves rather than what is done to us. Knowledge of our anatomy has grown tremendously since the olden days of quiltmaking. And with that, inevitably, comes a certain loss of innocence. We cannot just sit down to enjoy a cup of coffee anymore without an acute awareness of the damaging physiological effects of caffeine. There is no such thing as smoking a cigarette in peace. And though we still stuff ourselves with sweets and carbohydrates, while we sit in front of our television sets, we do so with some sense of nagging guilt. There is that inner voice that says we *do* know better. Then once the sugar blues hit, there is the resolution to diet, to go vegetarian, maybe even return to nature. Perhaps life was simpler when we didn't know any better. Today, however, we do. Some of the quilts were designed with those thoughts in mind.

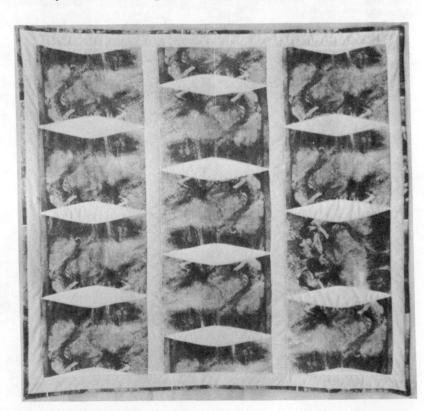

"Nuclear Power Plants"

Here is another version of "Back to Nature," first seen as a black and white drawing on page 29.

"TV" seemed to be an appropriate contrast to "Back to Nature."

39

The repetitive patterns of traffic can be an unending source of inspiration to the modern quiltmaker. Top left is "Crowded Parking Lot"; top right is "Parking Structure." Bottom is "One Way." On the facing page is a black and white drawing of a different version of the same pattern.

40

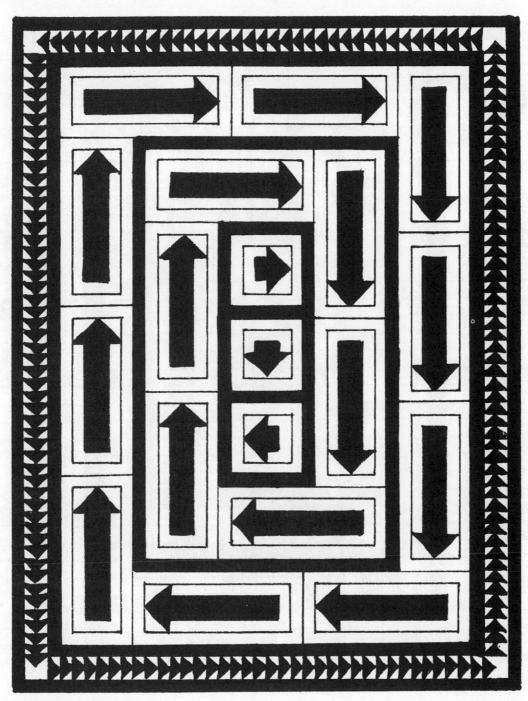

"One Way"

"Guardrail"

42

"Cloverleaf Expressway," another traffic-inspired design.

Here is another example of how a quilt pattern evolves. "Bicycle Wheels" is a design that was sparked by the sight of actual bicycle wheels hanging in a store window. (See below.)

The designing process began in a way similar to that of "No Deposit, No Return." First, the wheels were drawn realistically, with a design emerging very much like the traditional "Double Wedding Ring." As an experiment, I

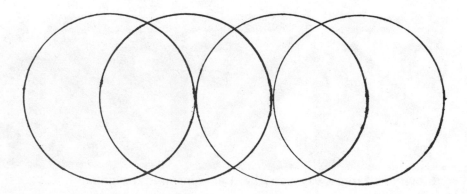

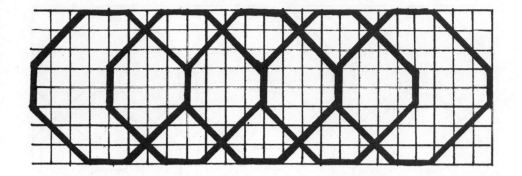

redrew this and altered it somewhat to fit, straightedged,
onto graph paper. Continuing to experiment, I drew this
pattern into rows, which formed an interesting overall effect.

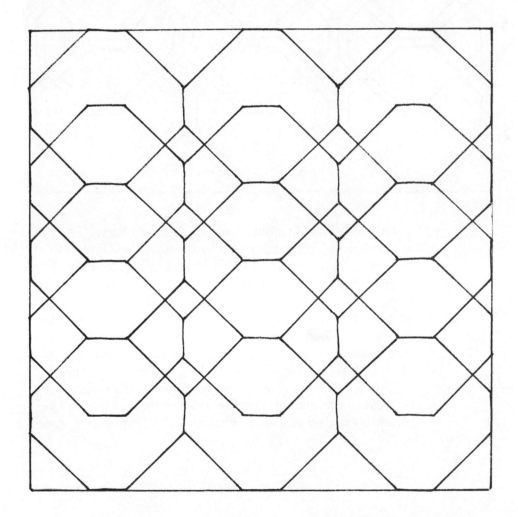

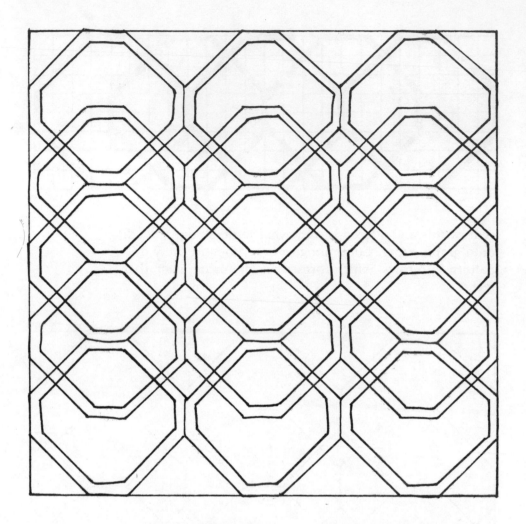

This idea was developed in two different ways: The first was a realistic approach to the subject matter. The basic geometric unit was outlined to resemble bicycle tires. The intersecting spokes could later determine the quilting pattern, helping to retain the original feeling of bicycle wheels. The second design is abstracted beyond the idea of wheels. It begins with the same basic geometric structure as in the first illustration but, with a different use of light and dark, a totally new feeling in design is created.

This is how one of my designs evolved. But, what is of interest to one person may be totally insignificant to another. By the same token, what excites one person's eye artistically may pass unnoticed by another's, because each person's sensitivity and creative process is different. With everyone's experiences and viewpoints being unique it's important to share, because through the sharing come new ideas. I hope that by sharing some of my thoughts, your own creative process will be stimulated to express what's important to you.

"Bicycle Wheels"—the final version.

"Save the Whales" can be
seen in color on the back
cover.

48

Personalizing Quilts

Not every woman who ever made a quilt was inspired with brilliant artistic vision or perfected sewing skills. Nevertheless, most quilts have become treasured heirlooms, for what may be lacking in artistic creativity is more than made up for in the personalized nature of each quilt. Though the same popular quilt designs have been recreated hundreds of times throughout the years, it is rare that two quilts are exactly alike. Fabric selection, color combinations, and design interpretations all contribute to the uniqueness of each quilt.

The memories stitched into quilts handed down to us through the generations have become as warm as the quilts themselves. Whether the quilt is in itself a beautiful artistic expression or just a warm bedcover, it takes on extra special meaning with the knowledge that father's old war uniform or baby's first dress are part of the creation. Quilts can be like family picture albums in the ways in which they preserve times past.

Signing and dating quilts became another personalizing aspect of the quiltmaking tradition. The quilter's name and date were often preserved by embroidery or india ink on a corner of the quilt. Some quilts were also named after their creators to continue for generations as family favorites. "Grandmother's Favorite" and "Aunt Sukey's Choice" are typical of quilt names that may very well have been named after a special person in someone's family.

Marriage and friendship or album quilts are highly individualized. Often the emphasis is more on expressions of sentimentality than on principles of design and color. For these quilts, each woman would design her own block, usually embroidering her name, the date, and adding, perhaps, a bit of poetry on it. The group would then meet to join the individually pieced blocks together and quilt the top as well. The completed quilt would be presented to the person it was created for, such as a bride-to-be, the minister, teacher, or some other deserving individual in the community.

As the hardships of the colonists and pioneers eased up and more time was available, the quilts developed into a source of pride for their makers. Women often kept a masterpiece quilt to work on, which was in a separate category from the everyday utility quilts. Masterpiece quilts were strictly for show, worked on only when they could be given the best of attention by their makers. Exhibits and contests rewarded those with the tiniest, most even stitches or the most intricate piecing. Some women would

What could be a more loving gift than a "Name Quilt"?

even secretly take out the stitches someone else might have put into their quilt, if they felt the stitches were less than perfect.

However, in addition to the showing off of skills and patience, quilting also became an expression of caring about the person the quilt was intended for. The time invested in a patchwork quilt is so great that the work could only be translated into a "labor of love."

The personalizing of quilts today is both an expected continuation of the tradition and a logical reaction to the mass-produced sameness of most of our products today. A natural extension of this idea is to incorporate into the actual design something of special significance to the person the quilt is intended for. Hopefully the following quilts will serve as a point of departure for expressing your own individuality.

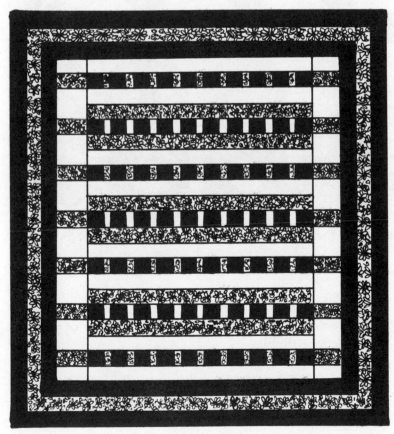

"Harmonica" is one of several I did with a musical motif.

Above is another "musical" quilt called "Banjo." On the opposite page is "Musicians' Quilt," which combines a number of musical motifs.

53

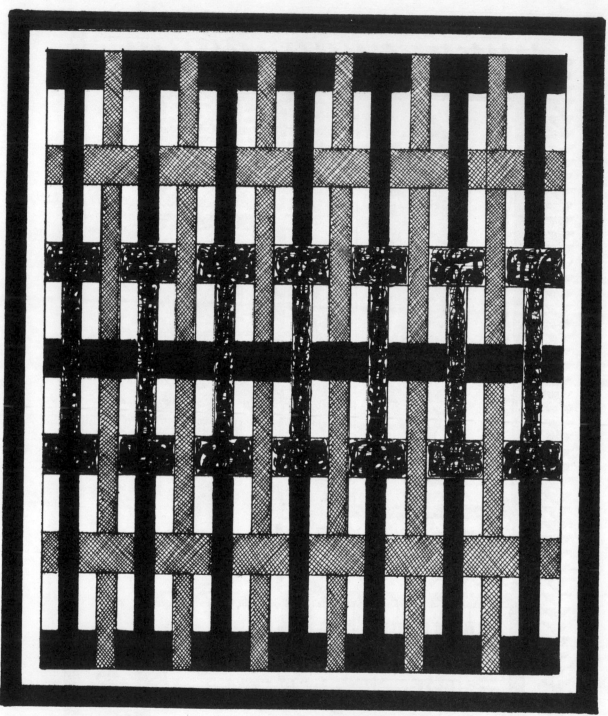

"Gavel Quilt" for members of the legal profession

The "gavel" motif is again used above; this time as a border for "Library Shelves." At right is an attempt to humanize one of the less popular forms of identification, "Computer Card."

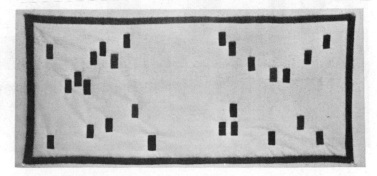

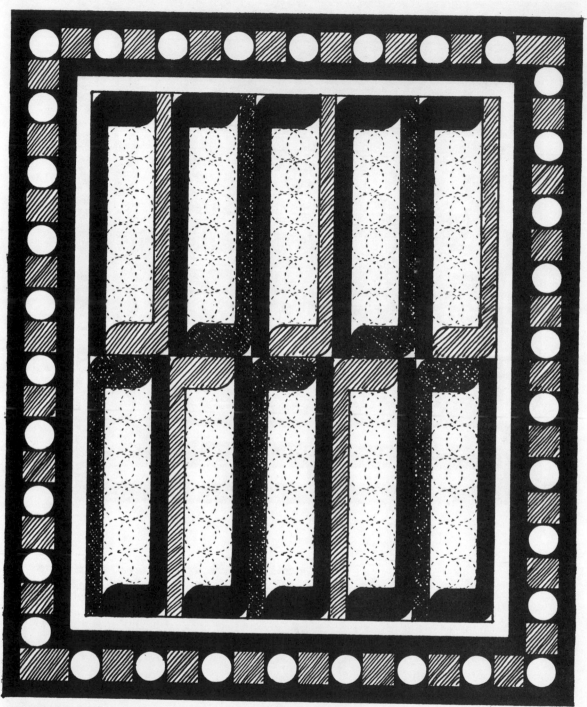

"Golfer's Quilt"

56

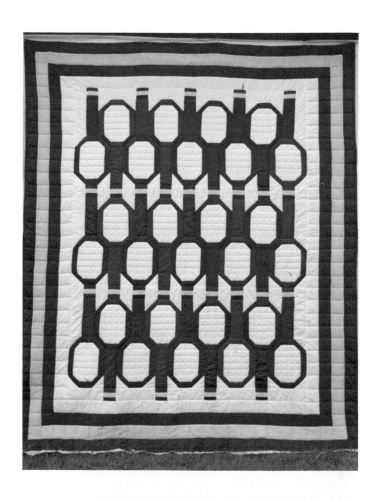

Sports and hobbies are excellent motifs for personalized quilts. On the opposite page, golf is celebrated. At top is "Tennis Anyone?" To the right is one for the film or camera enthusiast, "Aperture" with a "sprocket hole" border.

At left is the representational "Crossword Puzzle."

"Age of Aquarius," at left, is an updated "feather-edged star." This quilt is actually a re-creation of my own astrological chart, with the quilted and embroidered signs, degrees, planets, and phases of the moon, providing a new meaning to this old, but still lovely, design.

"Roller Skate Wheels"

Above are two "special interest" versions of the shelf motif: "Blue Jean Store Shelves," left, and "Bookshelves," at right. There is also still another black and white version of "Bookshelves" on the facing page.

At left is "Modern Architecture II." Modern Architecture III" and "Modern Architecture IV" are on pages 62 and 63.

"Library Bookshelves"

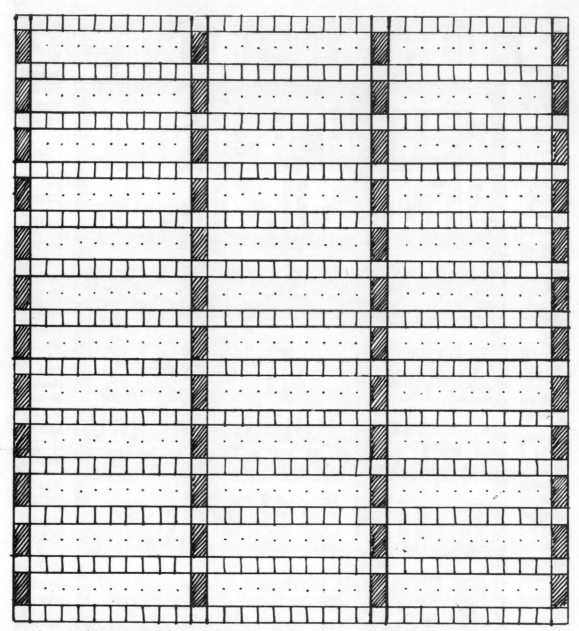

Modern Architecture III"

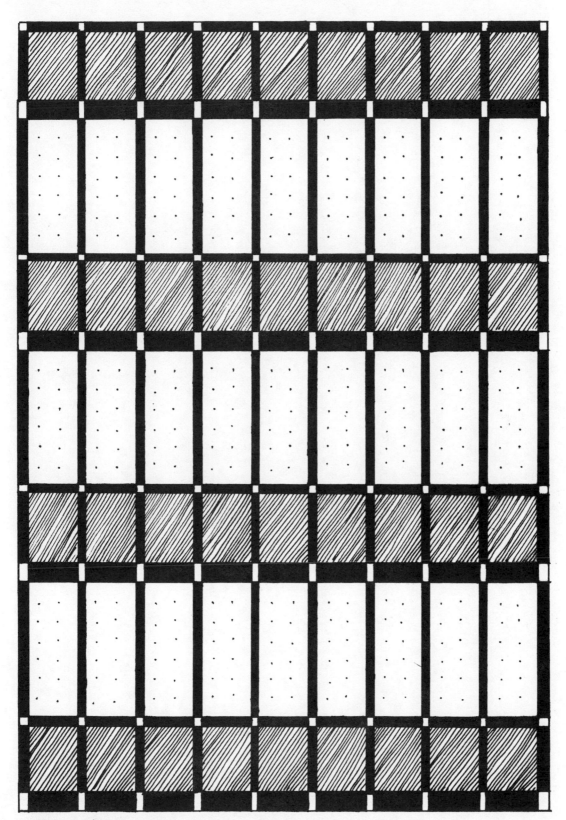

Modern Architecture IV"

To Make a Quilt

There are as many ways to make a quilt as there are people who make them. A technique one person swears by causes nothing but trouble for someone else and vice versa. Each teacher, how-to book, and quilter will have his or her own special way of doing things. Through the process of making a quilt, you also will develop your own style and techniques in both design and construction. However, it's useful to start out by learning some basics. The following how-tos of quiltmaking will help get you going.

templates

Making templates is the first step in quilt construction. A template is your pattern piece, cut out of cardboard or some other sturdy material, which will be your guide for cutting the pieces to your quilt. There are several different ways to make templates, depending on the particular pattern you have chosen.

For designs, using curved or irregular shapes, draw a single block of your quilt to actual size on graph paper. Duplicate in each square of the enlarged drawing exactly what you see in each square in your small drawing. (See the example on the next page.) Cut each differently shaped piece out of the graph paper, trace it onto light-weight cardboard or plastic, add a quarter of an inch to all sides (for seam allowances) and cut. Indicate which is the right side of irregularly shaped templates so that you do not inadvertently cut from the fabric a mirror image of your block.

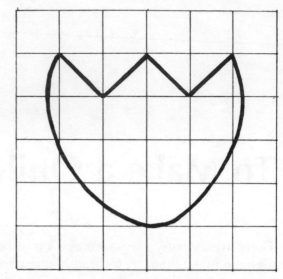

enlarging irregularly shaped pattern pieces

For patchwork patterns using only simple geometric shapes, there is no need to first draw the block to actual size. Just refer to your graph-paper drawing and do some simple multiplication. For example, in the finished "Cigarette" block on the opposite page, each square represents 1", so the "filter" will be 3" by 1" and the rest of the "Cigarette" 9" by 1". Adding ¼" to all sides of each pattern (for seam allowances) will make the templates 3½" by 1½" and 9½" by 1½".

Cardboard, plastic, and metal are all suitable materials for templates. If using cardboard, cut a duplicate. Eventually, the edges of the cardboard begin to wear out and before you know it, the template has changed sizes. Acetate (available in sheets from art supply stores) or plastics found around the house (coffee-can lids or the flat side of gallon milk containers) make good templates because the edges will not wear away. Metal templates are made in basic, standard shapes (available through quilting supply stores or mail order). They will come in handy for those who plan on making more than one quilt.

If you want to mark the seam lines on your fabric as well as the cutting lines, make a window template. To do so, first cut out the template as described previously. Then measure in towards the center of the template ¼" on all sides. Cut along this line with a matt knife. This should leave you a template with ¼" frame and a hollow inside.

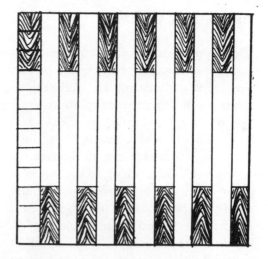

enlarging simple geometric patterns

The inside edge indicates your seam lines. A window template is also helpful when you want to see exactly what part of the print you will be cutting out.

It's absolutely essential that your templates are cut exactly. Even a fraction of an inch inaccuracy will make it difficult, if not impossible to match things up properly when piecing the blocks. Line the corners of the squares and rectangles up with the sharp edge of a table, counter, or T-square you know to be a perfect right angle and straight-edge to double-check the accuracy of your templates. And, of course, always make at least one practice block before undertaking the entire quilt.

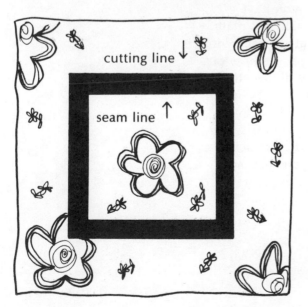

cutting line ↓

seam line ↑

window templates

estimating yardage

Once you have decided on a pattern and color scheme you must calculate how much of each chosen fabric you will need for your entire quilt. First, count the number of times each different template is used in one block. Multiply this by the number of blocks in your quilt.

To calculate how much of each different fabric you will need, figure how many times you can place your template along a 45" line (most fabric is 45" wide). You can do the figuring on paper or you can actually set the template along a tape measure to roughly estimate how many times it could be traced on that width of fabric.

For example, suppose you need 20 pieces, cut from a template 4½" square. I'd round that measurement up to 5" in my figuring to avoid working with fractions and to make sure that I had enough fabric. Always overestimate your fabric needs so that you have a bit extra to experiment with. Five goes into 45 nine times. A second row will allow me to cut out another 9. I would probably have enough material to get by for the two more needed (since I already had overestimated my needs by figuring the piece to be 5" instead of 4½"), but just to be certain, I'd buy enough fabric to allow for another row. I'd plan on buying at least 15" of 45" wide fabric for this one piece. Figure the remaining yardage needed in this way.

When you are using scraps of fabrics or clothing in your quilt, it is difficult to determine when you have enough. After some experience you can usually estimate visually the correct quantity. But for absolute certainty in the beginning, first cut out the chosen scraps, see how far they go, and then figure the yardage for the pieces still needed. This can be done only if your quilt is to be a blend of a great variety of prints, not just a select few. Also, when using an undetermined amount of fabric scraps, you'll probably plan and adjust your color scheme *after* you see how much of specific fabric types you actually have. (Usually, you'll want to have your color scheme worked out before you begin.)

fabrics

The best fabrics for patchwork and quilting are medium
dress- or shirt-weight 100 percent cottons. The fabric must
be soft so that you can maneuver a needle in and out of it
easily, but at the same time it must have a firm weave.
Loose weaves are not as durable and tiny quilting stitches
may not always take hold.

There are many other types of fabric available, but
there are things to be aware of about them. Cotton/poly-
ester blends are acceptable, but quilting stitches are easier
to make and nicer looking on 100 percent cotton. Thin,
sheer fabrics wear out quickly, making them an impracti-
cal choice for your quilt. Knits are too stretchy, and, in
general, just don't *look* as good as cottons in a finished
quilt. Velvets, satins, and similar slippery, tricky-to-work-
with fabrics should also be avoided. Quilts made of wool,
corduroy, denim, and the like are suitable when there is
no small, intricate piecing or quilting. ("Blue Jean Store
Shelves" is one such quilt, made from corduroy and old
jeans, tied together with yarn.)

Very interesting and beautiful effects can be obtained
by experimenting with fabrics—combining different
weights and textures. The blending of differing fabrics
[into one work is particularly well suited for wall hangings,] appliquéd or pieced in a free, nonexacting form.
However, for functional pieced quilts of the traditional
sort, it is best to use fabrics of the same, medium weight.

Make it a practice to preshrink all of your fabric, re-
gardless of whether it was purchased new or obtained sec-
ondhand. It makes sense to test the durability and washa-
bility of the fabric *before* it is made into your quilt. Most
fabrics today are colorfast. However, if you have a ques-
tionable material, place a swatch of it in hot water for an
hour. Occasionally stir the water. If the water changes
color, you can soak the fabric in water, heated on the
stove with a few tablespoons of vinegar, which sets the
dye. Then machine-wash it in hot water with a swatch of
white fabric. If it is still white after the washing, the dye is
set and safe for use.

The fabric used for the back of your quilt must also be
soft and of medium weight. Whether solid or print, it
should complement the colors on top. Therefore, you may

want to purchase the backing at the same time you purchase fabric for the top. Bed sheets are also suitable for backing a quilt.

cutting out

Iron your fabric and place it wrong-side-up on a table or cutting board. Sometimes after washing, it may be a bit stretched out. Gently pull it back into shape, ironing if necessary so that the grains line up with the edges of a square. Do not use the binded edges (selvages) of the fabric. They are slightly tighter than the rest of the fabric and will not allow you to cut an accurately sized piece.

Place your template on the wrong side of the fabric with the longest side along the lengthwise grain. Diamonds and right-angle triangles should have two sides on the straight of the fabric, as shown. Be aware if your pattern changes shape by cutting out on the wrong side of the material. (With "McDonalds," there is only one template for the yellow arches, but one half of them are cut with the template face-up, and half with it face-down.) Also, if you are using a striped material, note which direction the stripes will be going when the block is pieced.

placement of templates on fabric

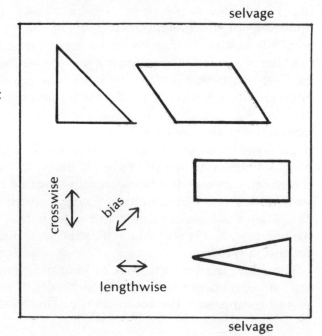

70

Trace along the edges of your template with the sharp point of a pencil or pen. Colored pencils, ballpoint pens, lead pencils, or dressmaker's chalk are all suitable—as long as the end result is a fine, sharply indicated cutting line. Thick, smudgy marks cause inaccurate cutting.

Using sharp, dressmaker's shears, cut your pieces out one at a time. It's tempting to pile several layers of fabric on top of each other to cut out at the same time, but it's almost impossible to end up with the underlying fabrics cut properly. Even if material is folded once, the bottom piece will probably not have been cut true to the straight of the grain. If pieces are cut on the bias, they will stretch out of shape, be difficult to fit neatly into the rest of the block, and will weaken the structure of the entire quilt.

Occasionally, instead of cutting, you can tear the fabric into the desired pieces, providing of course that it will not pucker or stretch out of shape. Cut the strips with a slightly larger than usual ¼″ seam allowance to compensate for unravelling. Make a few practice strips and measure them before going ahead with your whole project.

To cut all your fabric out before you begin piecing, or to do it block-by-block is a matter of personal preference. If, however, you doubt that there is enough of a certain fabric, which you absolutely need, cut it all out at once. Then if you need to buy more you can go right back to the store and, with luck, get more. Often, colors from different bolts of fabric will vary noticeably, even if the prints or solids are supposedly the same.

piecing

Piecing is the process of sewing together the individual pieces of fabric, cut with your templates, to form a block. The completed blocks are then joined or "set" together to complete your pieced patchwork top.

To begin, study your pattern to devise a piecing plan—an efficient, organized system for putting your block together. Look at the graph-paper drawing of your pattern and divide it into smaller sections first. Then join the small pieced sections together to form a complete block.

"Crossword Puzzle," a block consisting of 1″ squares, provides an example. (The illustration can be seen on the following page.) Do not sew the 13 squares across, attach-

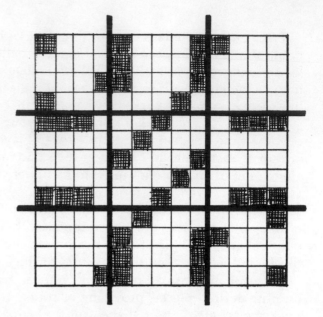

piecing plan for "Crossword Puzzle"

ing them to another row of 13. Rather, divide the block into smaller squares. This is the piecing plan: To sew a row of 4 squares, stitch it to another row of 4 squares until you have a square 4 rows long. Complete the other eight small sections before joining them all together. Piece each block of your quilt using the same system.

Place the two pieces of fabric to be joined, right sides together. Pin them in place if they are more than several inches long. When piecing diamonds or triangles, the points will extend out ¼" (the width of the seams). If sewing two bias edges together, they will probably stretch out of shape. To avoid this, pin the pieces securely, every inch or so. Better yet, try to avoid the situation altogether by having the edge of at least one of the pieces cut on the

piecing diamonds

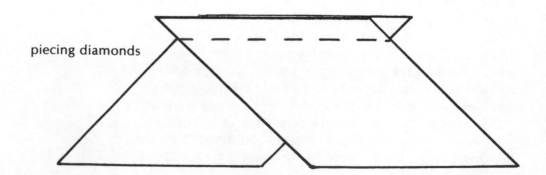

72

grain. To piece curves, first mark the centers of both curves. Stay-stitch along the seam line and clip. Match the centers. Stitch, beginning in the middle of the curve. Press.

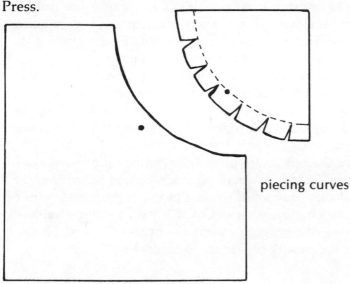

piecing curves

Make all seams ¼". If you are even slightly inaccurate, it will be difficult to get your blocks to lay flat and there will be puckers or stretching when setting them together later on. Mark seam lines in pencil if it helps you to be consistent.

Piecing can be done by hand or by machine. Long, straight seams are easiest and most practical to do by machine. They will generally be stronger than if done by hand. Small seams, curves, and awkward angles may sometimes be pieced more accurately by hand, using a tiny running stitch. If your pattern happens to be a tricky one, experiment on your practice block to see which method you prefer.

running stitch

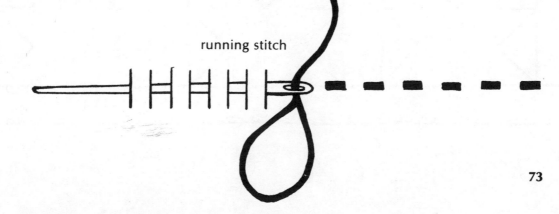

ironing

Ironing is very important to the overall neatness of your quilt. Do not wait until your block is complete to iron it. Rather, press each step of your construction before going on to the next. Press seams to one side or the other, not open, because that tends to weaken them.

If you press the seams of one row to the right and the next to the left, it becomes easier to match seams up when pinning the rows together. However, if you are using light-colored fabric through which you can see the seam, press the seam towards the darker fabric.

Once the blocks are pieced they must be pressed again or "sized." Mark a square on your ironing board the size your block is supposed to be. Pin the corners and sides of your block to this square. Cover it with a damp cloth and press, from the edges towards the center. This will help ensure uniformity of size in your blocks.

sashing

Sashing refers to strips of fabric sometimes sewn to the four sides of a block. These "lattice strips" are usually 2–5 inches wide and are used to set off blocks in a quilt like a frame.

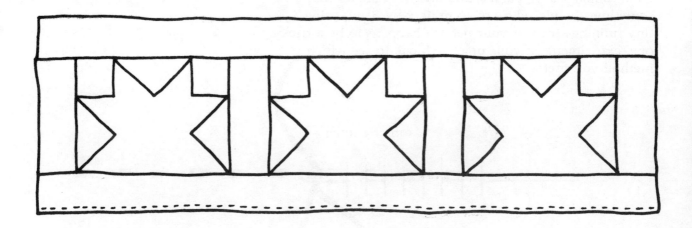

First, join the short lattice strips to two sides of your completed blocks, making a row. When you have two rows, join them with a long strip. There won't be seam lines to match here, so double-check to see that the blocks are vertically aligned with each other. Or else, join the short strips with squares. This will provide seam lines to match up, making it easier to vertically align the blocks accurately.

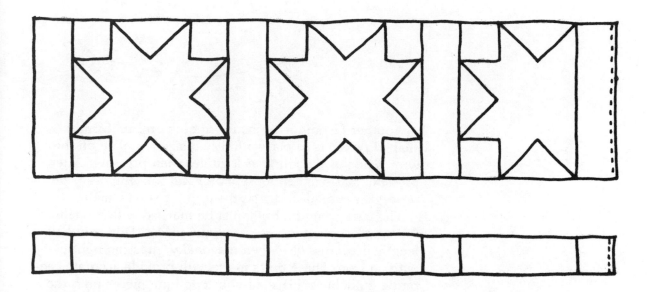

appliqué

Appliqué is a decorative sewing technique in which fabric cutouts are applied to a larger fabric background. This is different from piecing, where fabric pieces are sewn, right sides together, to form a design.

To appliqué, begin by following guidelines for making templates, preparing fabric, and cutting out as for piecing. Then, press ¼" seam allowances to the wrong side of each fabric cutout. With curved edges, first stay-stitch along the ¼" seamline by machine. Clip almost to the seamline. The sharper the curve, the closer together the clips should be. This will help keep the curves smooth. (See illustration on next page.)

75

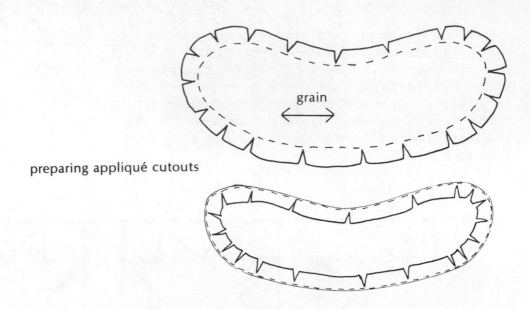

preparing appliqué cutouts

Another technique to insure smooth and uniformly shaped pieces is to place a finished size template on the wrong side of the fabric as a guide when pressing. After pressing, baste (stitch loosely by hand for temporary purposes) the turned-under seams in place. Press again.

The background fabric must be marked with guidelines for the placement of your appliqué pieces. Fold it in half lengthwise, crosswise, then diagonally, pressing lightly with an iron. These press marks will provide accurate centering guidelines. Place all your appliqué pieces onto the background fabric before stitching. If one piece is placed partially over another, that underneath part will not have to be stitched down. At these places, turn the seam allowance back out flat so as to avoid bumps. (See picture on opposite page.) If you want parts of your design raised, place a piece of quilt batting of the proper shape under that section. Pin, then baste all pieces down before stitching. Bias tape is used for stems or long, thin designs.

A slipstitch or blind stitch are the traditional techniques for securing appliqué pieces to the background. Use thread of the same color as the cutout, trying to make the stitches as invisible as possible, ⅛″ to ¼″ apart. Pieces can also be appliquéd by machine using about a 12-inch length stitching close to the edge of the shape. Instead of backstitching on the machine at the beginning and end, draw the top thread to the underside and tie. This will eliminate noticeable bumps of stitching.

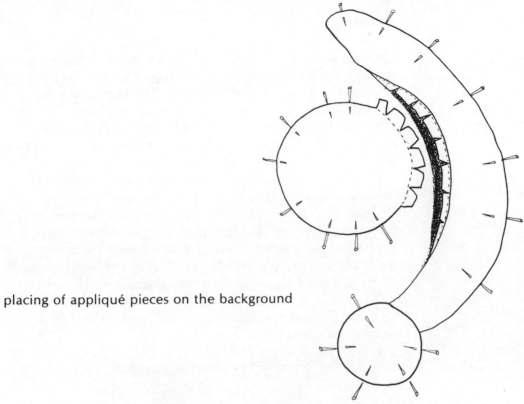

placing of appliqué pieces on the background

Embroidery stitches (such as the buttonhole stitch), either by hand or machine, and zigzag are other ways to attach your appliqué pieces to the background. (See below.)

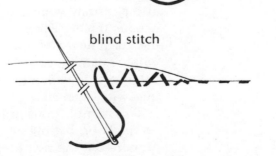

slipstitch

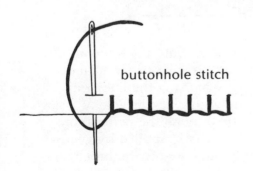

buttonhole stitch

blind stitch

77

quilting

Quilting is the process of stitching, by hand or machine, through the backing, batting, and top of a quilt for both decorative and functional purposes. The raised and depressed areas created by the quilting adds a beautiful third dimension to your work. It keeps the three layers securely together, preventing the batting from shifting and bunching. Quilting also keeps in warmth.

Mark out your quilting design onto the top either before assembling it into a frame, or afterwards. For outline quilting you can simply follow the lines of what you have pieced without marking it. Other quilting designs, however, must be marked in using dressmaker's chalk or a washable but sharp marking pencil. A sharp lead pencil is all right if used lightly because the quilting stitch, which will be done right on the line, will cover it. If it's too dark or thick, the pencil marks may show through and be difficult to wash out.

outline quilting

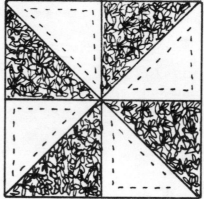

Trace intricate quilting patterns onto the top with a tracing wheel and dressmaker's tracing paper. You can also perforate your pattern by piercing the lines with a needle, tracing wheel, or the unthreaded needle of a sewing machine. Mark the fabric through the perforations with cinnamon, cornstarch, or chalk, applied by gently rubbing it in with a bit of batting. Reinforce these markings with a pencil.

To assemble your quilt, place the backing (face-down) on the floor, batting next, then the pieced top (face-up). Smooth out the wrinkles of all three layers as you lay them out. Be gentle with the batting so as not to tear it. The backing should extend a few inches beyond the top on all sides. Trim the batting even with the top.

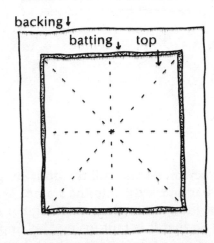

backing↓

batting↓   top

assembling the three layers of your quilt

Temporarily secure the three layers in place. Long dressmaker's pins are adequate, but are apt to fall out along the way, especially if you are constantly repositioning it in a hoop. Basting your quilt together is more work but it is also more reliable. Begin in the middle, stitching or pinning out to the sides, then again from the middle out, diagonally to the corners. You'll probably have to crawl onto the quilt to get at the middle; so make sure you straighten out any wrinkles you may have created. Double-check the backing so as not to baste in a pucker.

quilting in a frame

A quilting frame is a wooden structure used to mount a quilt and keep it taut while it is being quilted. A homemade frame can easily be made by using 2-by-1 lumber, secured at right angles by C-clamps, mounted on chairs or sawhorses. Frames are also available ready-made.

While the quilt is still on the floor, lay one of the two long bars of the frame along the top edge of the quilt. Both bars should have a strip of heavy fabric (denim or ticking) tacked or stapled along it. Secure the top edge of the quilt to this fabric. Use heavy thread and stitch across by hand several times so it will hold fast when stretched.

79

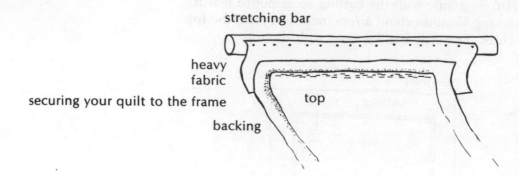

stretching bar

heavy
fabric

securing your quilt to the frame

top

backing

With another person's help, roll the quilt snugly and evenly onto the bar and set it into the frame. Then secure the other edge of the quilt to the remaining bar as before. Stretch the quilt so that it is taut (using C-clamps, pegs, gears, or whatever your frame has to offer), but not so taut that it's difficult to work a needle through it. Stretch the width of the quilt to the short sidebars of the frame with strong thread or seam binding. Begin quilting at the end, rolling up what you have completed as you go along. Another method of assembling your quilt in the frame is to roll half of it on one bar, half on the other. Begin at the middle of your quilt, working towards one end or the other. Then reroll the completed side, and begin at the middle again, working towards the other end.

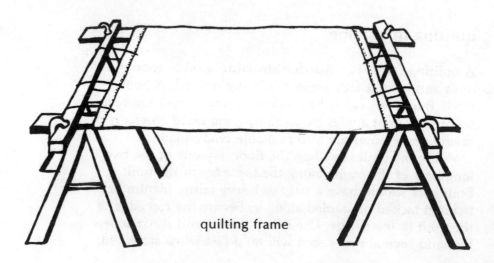

quilting frame

quilting in a hoop

Place the center of your basted quilt in a large circular hoop. Gently pull out the wrinkles on both the top and back so it is comfortably stretched. Quilt from the center of the hoop out. When you reposition it, have a bit of what you just quilted appear in the hoop. This way you will be sure not to create unwanted puckers or fullnesses in either the top or back. Begin quilting where you left off. When you reach the edges of your quilt, use smaller embroidery hoops, secure the raw edges of the quilt with strong thread to the hoop, or baste additional, temporary strips of fabric to the raw edges of the top.

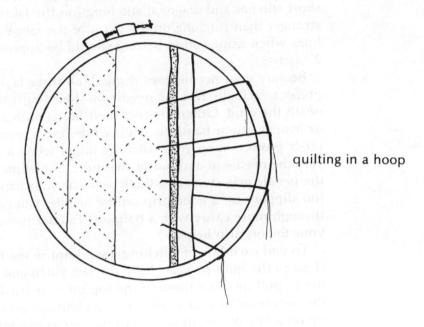

quilting in a hoop

the quilting stitch

To quilt, tie a knot at the end of a single thread (15″–20″ long). Use quilting thread which is stronger than regular thread and does not knot so easily. Pass the needle (short, sharp, size 8–10) from back to top, tugging gently 'til you feel the knot pop through the back. This is most easily done near a seam. Don't pull the knot through the top. This knot, locked in the batting, will keep your stitching from becoming undone.

81

Take 3–4 running stitches at a time along your marked lines, 5–10 stitches per inch. Ideally each stitch should be the same size as the spaces between them on both the top and the back. Another sign of fine quilting is when the beginnings and endings of a line of stitching are indiscernable. However, quilting is a skill that takes time to develop. There's no reason to be frustrated if your stitches are a bit uneven or irregular. These are goals to work towards—not a realistic starting point.

With the modern polyester batting available today, there is no longer the need to quilt every inch or so of the top as in the old days. You can allow 7–9 inches of unquilted space without the batting shifting or bunching with use and washings. However, in general, the closer your quilting lines, the stronger your quilt will be. Also, short stitches and diagonal stitching (on the fabric bias) is stronger than stitching on the grain of the fabric. Quilting lines when using cotton batting should be approximately 2" apart.

Be sure your needle goes through all three layers. Some prefer to actually feel the needle on their finger underneath the quilt. Others protect their finger with a rubber or leather cap or bandage. Meanwhile, use a thimble or other protection on your stitching finger while it maneuvers the needle in and out of the quilt. Sometimes when the needle gets stuck in a thick seam or your hands get too slippery for a good grip on the needle, you can pull it through more easily with a balloon. Talcum powder on your fingers also helps.

To end each line of stitching, tie a knot in the thread close to the quilt surface. Take the last stitch and gently tug to pull the knot through the top into the batting. Run the needle an inch or so through the batting, bringing it up on a line of the quilting pattern. Try as much as possible to hide where your quilting begins and ends. You can also finish with one or two even backstitches (if you don't mind them showing).

tufting

Tufting is a way to hold a quilt together by tying double knots of thread or yarn through all three layers at regular intervals. These are then called tied or tacked quilts.

Lay the three layers of your quilt smoothly on the floor or over a long table. You needn't assemble it in a frame or hoop for tufting, but be careful to avoid wrinkles or puckers in the backing. With a large-eyed needle, double-threaded with knitted worsted or embroidery floss, push the needle from the top of the quilt to the bottom, leaving 4–5" of thread on top. Come up from the back, approximately ½" from the first thread. Repeat, pushing the needle down, then back up in the same holes. Tie the ends of yarn in a square knot and clip them to approximately 1–2".

apartment quilting

Apartment quilting is a space-saving method of assembling your quilt whereby each block is quilted separately before it is set together with the rest. Individual blocks can be quilted by machine or by hand. In either case, cut the batting and backing evenly with the block. The blocks can be basted (from the center out to the sides and diagonally), but this is not always necessary.

For hand-quilting, stretch your block in a quilting hoop or a small frame. An easily adjustable frame can be made by four pieces of 2-by-1 lumber, held together at the corners by C-clamps. Stretch, and attach the edges to the frame with pushpins. Quilt from the center out.

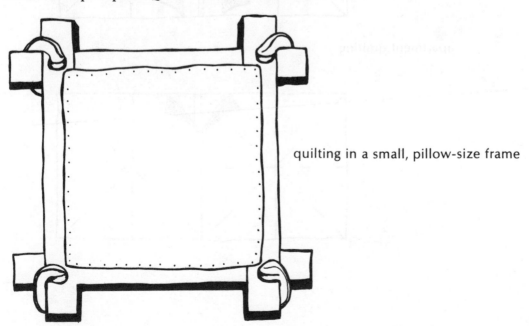

quilting in a small, pillow-size frame

For machine quilting, stretch your block in an embroidery hoop so that the fabric lies flat against the surface of the sewing machine. You can also machine quilt without a hoop. In either case, experiment with stitch length, pressure, and tension settings. Practice stitching your quilting pattern before you attempt your actual project because machine quilting can be a tricky maneuver.

Leave at least ½″ around the edge of the blocks unquilted so that you can attach them together smoothly. Join two quilted blocks with a ¼″ seam, stitching (by machine or hand) only the tops. See that the batting pieces overlap approximately ¼″. Then turn the backing under ¼″ and join the two sections with a slipstitch. Continue adding blocks to form rows. Join the rows in the same way.

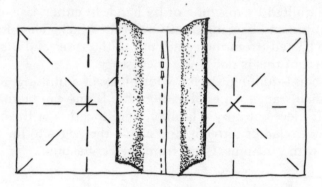

apartment quilting

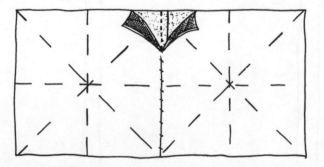

one-step piecing/quilting

Quilts formed from strips of fabric can be pieced and
quilted in one and the same step. ("Cigarette" was put together in this way.) To begin, lay out the backing and batting (cut about 1" larger on all sides than the top of your
block-to-be). Place your first two strips, right sides together, approximately 1" from the left edge of the batting
and backing. Stitch through all layers, leaving ½" at the
top and bottom of the strips free. Open the second strip
so that its right side is up and press. Lay the third strip on
the second, right sides together as before. Stitch, open,
and press. Continue in this way to build your individual
blocks. Join the completed blocks as for "apartment quilting."

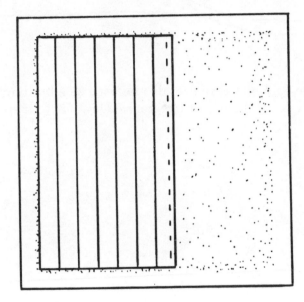

one-step piecing/quilting

binding

A binding is the narrow border along the outer edges of
the quilt that closes up the raw edges. It is the last step in
completing your quilt.

To bind, trim the backing on all sides ¾" to 1¼" larger
than the quilt top. Quilt top and batting should be even.
Turn under ¼" and fold over to the top of the quilt. Have
the quilt top marked in pencil ¼" along the edges. Pin to
the pencil marks on the quilt top, beginning at the center,

working towards the corners. Machine stitch close to the edge, or slipstitch in place, again beginning at the center.

Another method of binding is to cut strips of fabric 2″–5″ wide. Trim all three layers of your quilt so that they are even. Pin the binding, right sides to the quilt top and stitch in place (most practically by machine) through all three layers. Turn under the free edge ¼″, then turn it over the raw edges of the quilt to the back, pinning it in place just over the line of machine stitching. Slipstitch in place.

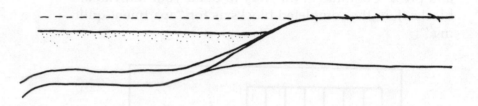

Double-fold bias tape can also be used as a binding, especially for scalloped or irregular edges, where there is a need for stretch.

Plans and Patterns

The following pages contain plans and notes for the construction of each design. Dimensions given for pattern pieces are of the finished size; seam allowances are not included.

Save the Whales is both pieced and appliquéd. The center portion of the square is pieced so that the body of the "whale" lines up properly with the surrounding "water." The rest of the pieces are appliquéd in a free-form style, with no exact piecing plan to follow.

back cover and page 48

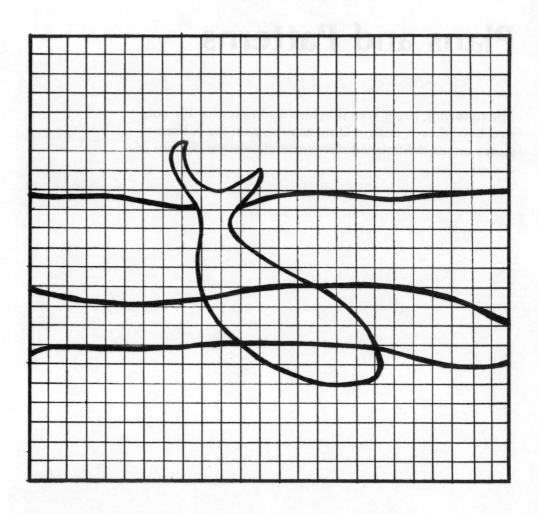

Solar Energy is an appliqué design. Six full circles, each approximately 2″ larger than the next are sewn on top of each other (rather than cutting the fabric pieces to the exact moon-shaped sizes).

page 1

Lifesavers is tricky to piece because of the curves. Each block should be sized, using an iron, to make sure that all the blocks are the same size, before setting them together. It is pieced in four sections, finishing 8″ square.

page 2

No Deposit, No Return is an easy one to piece, requiring only two pattern pieces. First, attach the "caps" to the "bottles." Then join the bottles, upside-up, upside-down, and so forth.

page 19

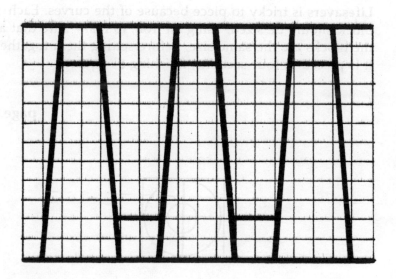

Product Code is built from rows of 11" strips, of widths varying from ½" to 2".

page 19

Hamburgers is approximately 9" long, 7¾" wide, with a 2½" layer of red, yellow, and brown strips between the "buns." It is appliquéd onto an 11½" background with a 2" border. A long green strip is gathered and stitched over the layer of three colored strips for the "lettuce."

page 20

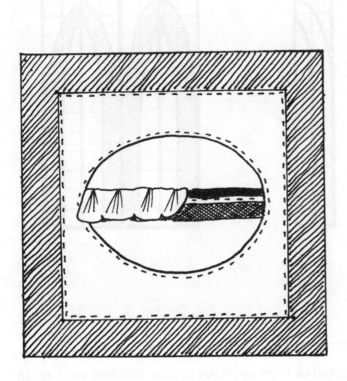

McDonald's Arches contain single squares of 12" x 8". Each arch is built from two sections, 12" x 2" (containing three different pattern pieces each) and two mirror sections.

page 20

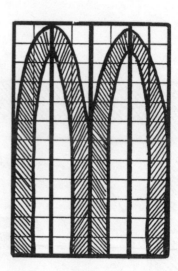

Vegetarian is an appliqué design, stitched onto an 18" background with a 3" border. Here, as with many of the designs, the fabric was chosen especially to enhance the particular theme of the quilt. In this case, the border fabric is a print of fruits and vegetables.

page 21

"Rock 'n Roll"

On opposite page is a drawing on graph paper of "Sun Blossoms."

At right is "Tract Homes." Left below is "Expressway." At right below is "Red Tape."

"Born Again"

The twenty blocks in this sampler are examples of the hundreds of traditional patchwork patterns that were inspired by some aspect of the makers' lives. From the top left, reading across, the names of the individual blocks are "Weathervane," "Indian Hatchet," "Road to California," "Wild Goose Chase," "Snail's Trail," "Maple Leaf," "Goose Tracks," "Broken Dishes," "Windmill," "Cactus Flower," "Moon over the Mountain," "Dresden Plate," "Anvil," "Bear's Paw," "House on the Hill," "Churn Dash" (also known as "Lover's Knot"), "Log Cabin," "Bow Ties," "Spools," and "Flock of Geese."

Dieter's Fruit Plate is an appliqué design stitched onto an 18″ background. The "bananas" are lined so that the darker colors of the "apples" and "oranges" do not show through.

page 21

Morning Coffee has a 6″ square for its body. The "handle" is built from 2″ squares and triangles. The "mugs" are set together with 2″ wide lattice strips. Quilting is diagonal along the lattice strips.

page 22

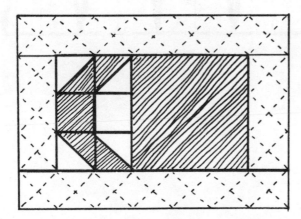

Sugar Blues is pieced in rows. There are two different rows. The bottom row in the piecing-plan diagram is the same as the top, just pieced upside down. The middle row is pieced from a single shape, set right side up, then up side down, and so forth.

page 22

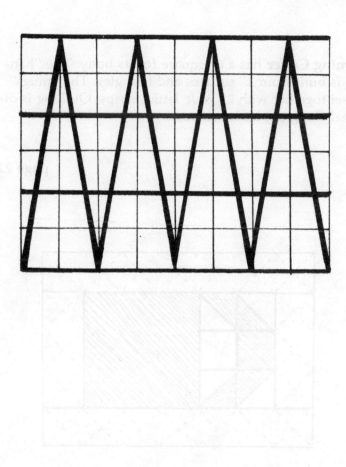

98

Cigarettes is made using the one-step piecing/quilting method. First, the "filter" (1" x 3") is pieced to the rest of the "cigarette" (1" x 9"). The strips are then joined together to form a block 12" x 12". Completed blocks are joined using the method as described in the section on apartment quilting.

page 22

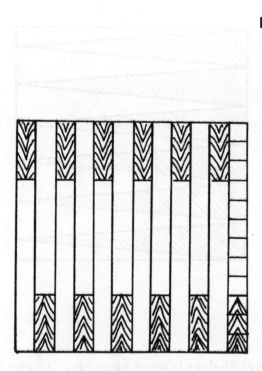

Backgammon's piecing plan shows ¼ (12″) of a baby-size quilt. There is a 2″ border on all sides except for the central strip, separating the right from the left, which is 3″. The border is of a single triangle, 3″ high with a 2″ base.

page 23

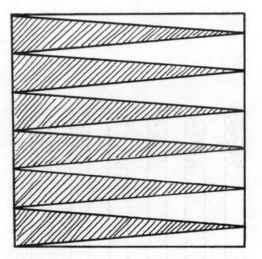

Supermarket Shelves is more of an idea sampler than a single, finished, patchwork pattern. It demonstrates the numerous pleasing, repeatable shapes to be found on supermarket shelves. Any one of them (and in many combinations) could be used as the basis for a patchwork pattern.

pages 24, 25, and 26

Potted Plants requires a combination of hand and machine sewing. The straight-seamed design formed by the pots can be pieced by machine. The plant leaves should be appliquéd by hand, using bias seam tape for the winding stem.

page 27

Back to Nature is pieced in five rows. Although the piecing is easy, there are seventeen different pattern pieces to keep track of. All the seams are straight except for the piece in the middle row next to the roof which has one odd angle. This seam should be clipped so it will lie smoothly.

pages 29 and 39

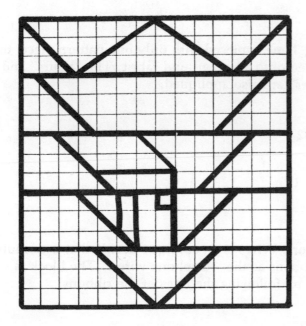

Sidewalk Bricks are 9½" x 4¼" pieces, separated by 1½" lattice strips. When joining the long rows of "bricks," be sure to double-check that they are aligned properly because there will not be seam lines to match up.

page 30

Inflation is a design of expanding squares and rectangles, pieced in rows.

page 31

Passing Time is pieced with only one pattern piece, then appliquéd onto a background fabric. The "hours" and "minutes" are also appliquéd.

page 32

Telephone Wires is an appliqué design that uses multicolored ribbons as the "telephone wires." The block is quilted by following the lines of the ribbons.

page 33

Winter Tree is different from most of the other designs in that it is not a single pattern repeated over and over. Rather it is a single form that continually changes and develops as it grows. It is designed to be pieced entirely by using only small squares and triangles. However, the same tree shape could be appliquéd in a free form style. Snow flakes could be pieced or quilted onto the background fabric, with layers of "snow" appliqued onto the branches.

page 34

Spring Flowers can be pieced entirely by machine. First, piece each single blossom, then join them in rows, and attach each row to the completed rows of stems and leaves.

page 35

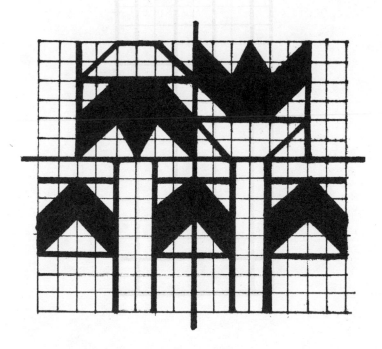

Modern Architecture is a concept that can provide almost unlimited opportunities for patchwork designs. Here are some of mine. All of the patterns can be adjusted easily for pillows, wall hangings, or full-sized bed quilts.

Modern Architecture I, page 36

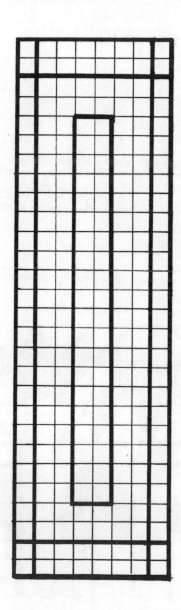

Modern Architecture II, page 60

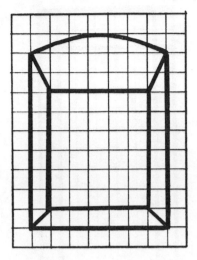

Modern Architecture III, page 62

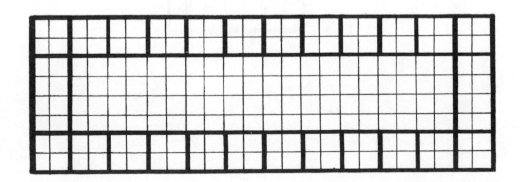

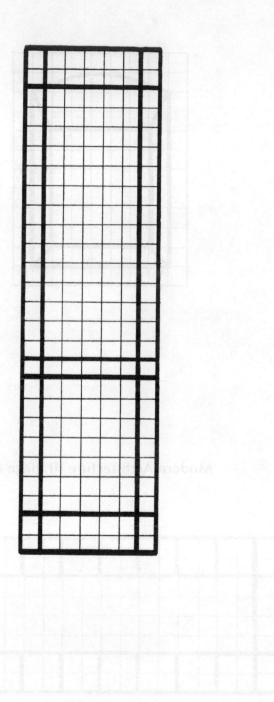

High-rise Apartments is a straight-seamed design, which uses "Sidewalk Bricks" as a border.

page 37

Nuclear Power Plants is simple to piece, despite the curves. It is pieced in rows separated by 1½" white strips. Clip the curved seams.

page 38

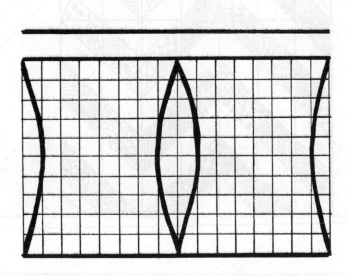

TV uses only right triangles sewn together to form 2″ squares. The corner squares are appliquéd onto 2″ squares of fabric, the same as are used for the 4″ wide border so as to resemble an actual TV set more clearly.

page 39

Parking Structure is a repeated series of four long, separated rows.

page 40

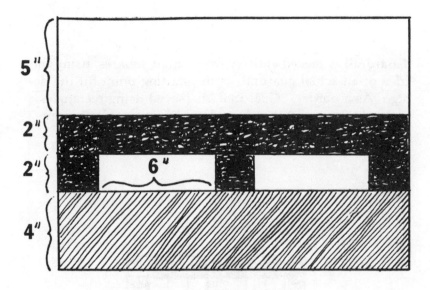

Crowded Parking Lot is pieced in rows of "cars" separated by 1" strips. Every two rows of cars are separated by 4". Each car is a 2" square, with 1" rectangles sewn to either side. Piece in small sections.

page 40

Bumper-to-Bumper (the border of "Crowded Parking Lot") is a continuous line of "cars," 2" squares with two 1" strips sewn to either side. The 1" pieces should be of the same color; either matching, or complementing the center 2" square, so as to more realistically resemble actual cars.

One Way consists of an arrow, 2" x 9", with a tip built from four 2" right triangles. Two 1" borders of contrasting colors surround the arrow. Can also be done as a larger piece.

pages 40 and 41

Guardrail is pieced entirely from small squares, using the idea of an actual guardrail as the starting point for the design. As a border, "Guardrail" is pieced using rectangles instead of squares, thereby resembling a guardrail more realistically.

page 42

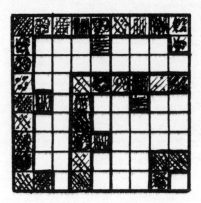

Cloverleaf Expressway is made entirely from 2″ squares and right triangles. The only difficult aspect to recreating this pattern is that with so many small pattern pieces, it is very easy to get the placement of light and dark mixed up. Therefore, as with most patchwork, it is important to piece the top in small sections.

page 43

Bicycle Wheels: Utilizing the following illustration as a starting point, you will find there are several approaches to the construction of this design. It can be pieced, using the pattern as outlined, or each of these shapes could be divided in half, thus eliminating the odd angles.

pages 44, 45, 46, and 47

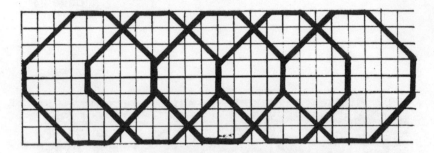

If a rim is to be added as in the next illustration, the entire row should be pieced in three separate sections.

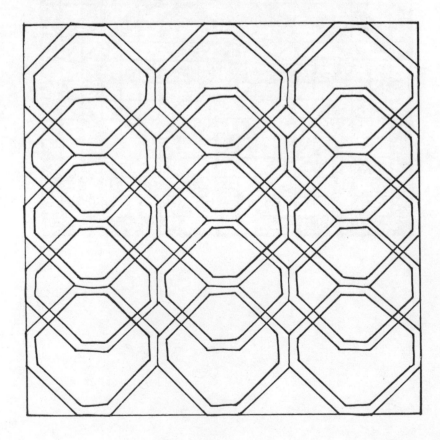

Name Quilt is built entirely from 1½″ squares. The first and last names are 4 squares high and wide. The middle-name letters were worked into a 3-square width because the name is relatively longer than the other two.

page 50

Harmonica consists of rows of small squares and rectangles. These can be constructed in either the traditional way of cutting out each piece separately before sewing them together, or by using the strip/piece method. In this method, long strips are sewn together, keeping the width of the squares and rectangles the same, thus all the rows are pieced at once, then cut into strips of the correct width.

page 51

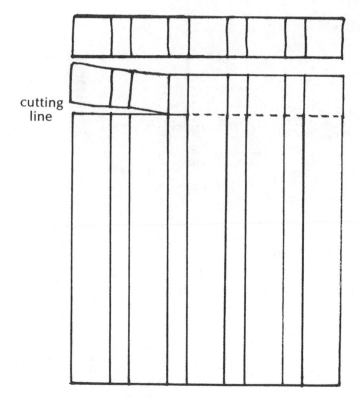

cutting
line

Banjos: A row of "banjos" is pieced in three horizontal sections. First, the heads of the banjos are pieced; then joined to the top of the banjo neck. The first and third rows are similar. The middle rows are simple vertical seams, joining the midsections of the banjo.

page 52

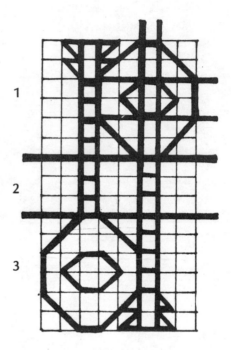

Musician's Quilt is similar to a traditional sampler, because there are many different blocks incorporated into one quilt. Music, of course, is the unifying theme. Both appliqué and machine piecing are used.

page 53

Gavel Quilt is all straight seams, pieced in horizontal rows.

page 54

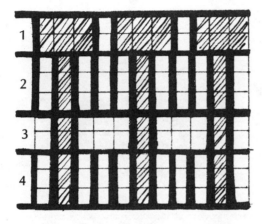

Library Shelves is pieced very much in the same way as "Bookshelves" except that it is quilted rather than knotted.

page 55

Computer Card is a free-form appliqué design. Small ¾" x 1½" fabric pieces are stitched onto a background and positioned in ways to suggest a computer card.

page 55

Golfer's Quilt is made with a combination of piecing and appliqué techniques. The base of a club is a single rectangle of fabric with two of the corners turned under in a curve, then appliquéd onto a small square of contrasting fabric. The "golf balls" along the border should also be appliquéd rather than pieced because they are so small.

A row of golf clubs should be pieced in three horizontal sections.

page 56

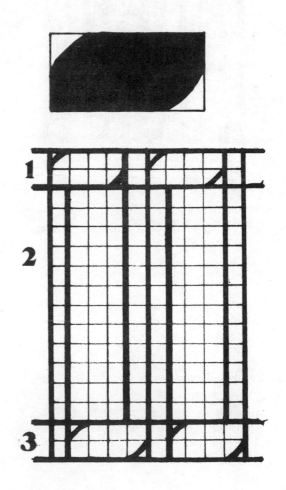

Tennis, Anyone? is pieced from a repeated series of three rows. Each square on the piecing plan represents 1½".

page 57

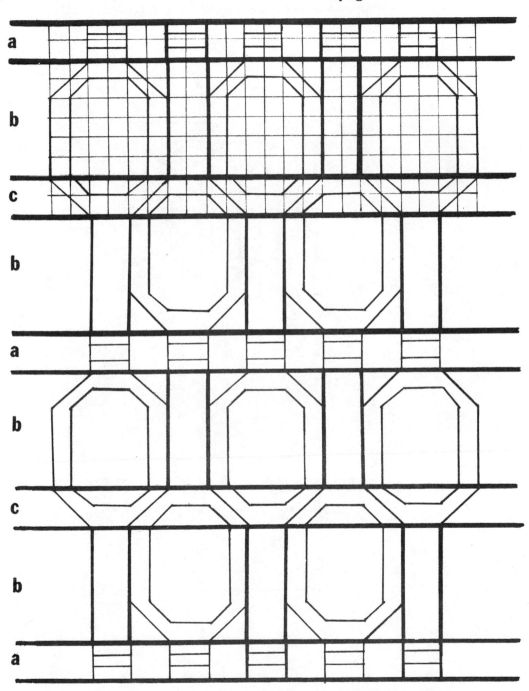

a

b

c

b

a

b

c

b

a

Aperture is similar to the traditional "Pinwheel" except for the varying sizes of the center "aperture" openings. Be careful that you do not inadvertently cut out a mirror image of your block. The pattern pieces will be of a different shape, depending on whether or not you trace it on the right side or the wrong side of the fabric.

page 57

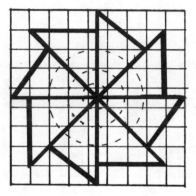

Sprocket Hole border is 4" x 1" dark strip, joined to a 1" square and repeated. There is a ½" strip sewn along each side.

Crossword Puzzle, shown here is just one of an endless variety of patterns to be created from the arrangement of single squares. The block is pieced in nine small sections.

page 58

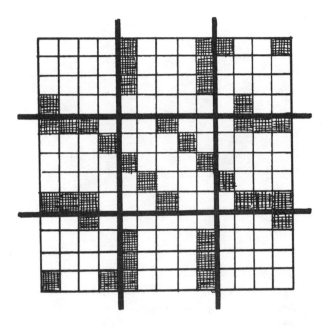

Age of Aquarius is based on the traditional "Feather-edged Star," with "Sawtooth" borders. The star can be easily divided into twelve sections, representing the twelve houses of an astrological chart. The signs, planets, and degrees are hand-embroidered. Quilting, depicting the phases of the moon, borders the center star. Planets and moons are appliquéd to the top and bottom edges with free-form quilting.

Roller Skate Wheels is relatively difficult to piece, as are all curved patterns. Another way to approach this design is to appliqué the curved pieces onto the corners of a square.

page 59

Blue Jean Store Shelves is 12″ x 2″ strips of old jeans separated by 2″ wide corduroy lattice strips. Because the corduroy and denim are such heavy fabrics, the quilt is tied together with yarn instead of quilting. The zigzag border is made from 2″ right triangles.

page 60

Bookshelves are multi-colored fabric strips, 7″ x 1″. Long, 1″ wide strips, one light, one dark, separate the rows of "books." It is tied with yarn, approximately every 3″.

pages 60 and 61

Rock 'n' Roll has two different squares, making up the overall design. The curved square can be pieced or appliquéd, depending on whether the pieces are large or small. The other part is simply a square, with a triangle sewn to each side.

page 93

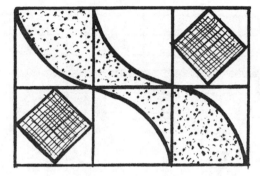

Sun Blossoms is an appliqué design, bringing together the rays of the sun with the flowers it nurtures for an effective summer theme quilt.

page 94

Tract Homes is built in rows; the "houses" and "tree trunks" are one row, the "leaves," "roofs," and "sky" form the second. A strip of blue is sewn to the top and bottom of these rows, joining them. "Doors" are appliquéd onto the houses' fronts.

page 95

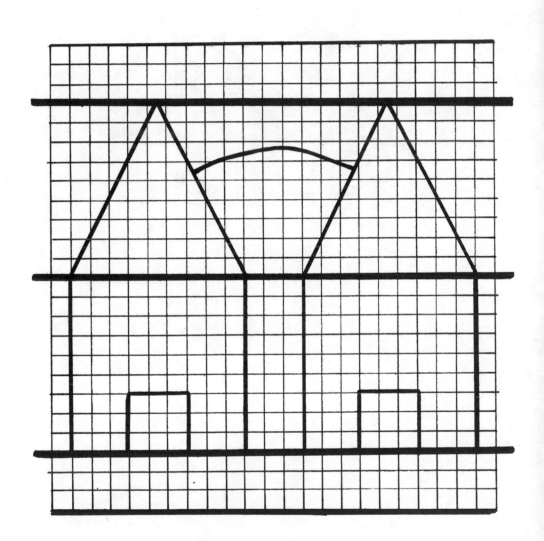

Expressway is a combination of "Bumper-to-Bumper" separated by tiny squares, sewn in strips, and with a "Guardrail" border.

page 95

Red Tape is both pieced and appliquéd. The long red strips are 1½" wide, separated by 3" sections of white. The curved ends of the rows are done separately. The curves are too tiny to piece, so they are appliquéd onto 1½" squares. The appliquéd squares are joined with 3" x 1½" white pieces to form two long, vertical strips. These long strips are finally joined to the midsection, matching seamlines.

page 95

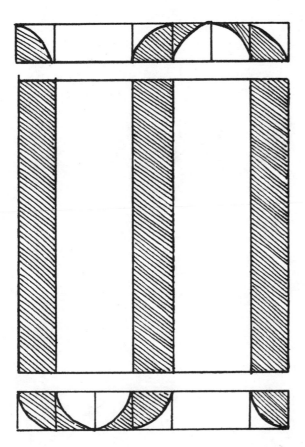

Born Again is a pieced design with a star/cross appliquéd onto it.

page 96

METRIC EQUIVALENCY CHART

CONVERTING INCHES TO CENTIMETRES AND YARDS TO METRES

mm — millimetres   cm — centimetres   m — metres

INCHES INTO MILLIMETRES AND CENTIMETRES
(SLIGHTLY ROUNDED FOR YOUR CONVENIENCE)

inches	mm		cm	inches	cm	inches	cm
⅛	3mm			7	18	29	73.5
¼	6mm			8	20.5	30	76
⅜	10mm	or	1cm	9	23	31	78.5
½	13mm	or	1.3cm	10	25.5	32	81.5
⅝	15mm	or	1.5cm	11	28	33	84
¾	20mm	or	2cm	12	30.5	34	86.5
⅞	22mm	or	2.2cm	13	33	35	89
1	25mm	or	2.5cm	14	35.5	36	91.5
1¼	32mm	or	3.2cm	15	38	37	94
1½	38mm	or	3.8cm	16	40.5	38	96.5
1¾	45mm	or	4.5cm	17	43	39	99
2	50mm	or	5cm	18	46	40	102
2½	65mm	or	6.3cm	19	48.5	41	104
3	75mm	or	7.5cm	20	51	42	107
3½	90mm	or	9cm	21	53.5	43	109
4	100mm	or	10cm	22	56	44	112
4½	115mm	or	11.5cm	23	58.5	45	115
5	125mm	or	12.5cm	24	61	46	117
5½	140mm	or	14cm	25	63.5	47	120
6	150mm	or	15cm	26	66	48	122
				27	68.5	49	125
				28	71	50	127

YARDS TO METRES
(SLIGHTLY ROUNDED FOR YOUR CONVENIENCE)

YARDS	METRES	YARDS	METRES	YARDS	METRES	YARDS	METRES	YARDS	METRES
⅛	0.15	2⅛	1.95	4⅛	3.80	6⅛	5.60	8⅛	7.45
¼	0.25	2¼	2.10	4¼	3.90	6¼	5.75	8¼	7.55
⅜	0.35	2⅜	2.20	4⅜	4.00	6⅜	5.85	8⅜	7.70
½	0.50	2½	2.30	4½	4.15	6½	5.95	8½	7.80
⅝	0.60	2⅝	2.40	4⅝	4.25	6⅝	6.10	8⅝	7.90
¾	0.70	2¾	2.55	4¾	4.35	6¾	6.20	8¾	8.00
⅞	0.80	2⅞	2.65	4⅞	4.50	6⅞	6.30	8⅞	8.15
1	0.95	3	2.75	5	4.60	7	6.40	9	8.25
1⅛	1.05	3⅛	2.90	5⅛	4.70	7⅛	6.55	9⅛	8.35
1¼	1.15	3¼	3.00	5¼	4.80	7¼	6.65	9¼	8.50
1⅜	1.30	3⅜	3.10	5⅜	4.95	7⅜	6.75	9⅜	8.60
1½	1.40	3½	3.20	5½	5.05	7½	6.90	9½	8.70
1⅝	1.50	3⅝	3.35	5⅝	5.15	7⅝	7.00	9⅝	8.80
1¾	1.60	3¾	3.45	5¾	5.30	7¾	7.10	9¾	8.95
1⅞	1.75	3⅞	3.55	5⅞	5.40	7⅞	7.20	9⅞	9.05
2	1.85	4	3.70	6	5.50	8	7.35	10	9.15

Index